Return to table of contents

Chapter 1: Doing Business In Morocco

- Market Overview
- Market Challenges
- Market Opportunities
- Market Entry Strategy

Market Overview Return to top

The U.S.-Moroccan Free Trade Agreement (FTA), which went into effect in 2006, is one of the most comprehensive free trade agreements that the U.S. has ever negotiated. Morocco is the second Arab and first African nation to have an FTA with the U.S. The FTA provides U.S. exporters increased access to the Moroccan market by eliminating tariffs on 95% of currently traded consumer and industrial goods and levels the playing field with European competition. It provides enhanced protection for U.S. intellectual property, including trademarks and digital copyrights, expanded protection for patents and product approval information and tough penalties for piracy and counterfeiting.

Morocco is steadily progressing toward greater internal modernization and globalization, with the creation of the country's first commercial courts, streamlined customs services and 16 Regional Investment Centers dedicated solely to facilitating new business ventures. In 2003, the Moroccan government passed a comprehensive labor code that protects both employers and employees.

Strategically located along the Strait of Gibraltar just a seven-hour flight from JFK and three hours from Paris, Morocco is seen more and more as a regional hub in North Africa for shipping logistics, assembly, production and sales. The moderate Mediterranean climate on 2,750 miles of coastline and its developing infrastructure make Morocco an attractive location for both business and leisure. Morocco's Association Agreement and Advanced Status with the European Union (EU) and the FTA with the U.S. have spurred development of manufacturing. Morocco relies on these key trade agreements to stimulate economic growth and to foster the job creation necessary to facilitate social and educational reform.

In the agricultural sector, Morocco is heading toward a good 2010-1 harvest. The record rain registered during the fall and early winter should lead to good yields in 2011. Morocco relies on imports to fulfill local demand for wheat. Morocco is the size of California, but only 20% of the land is arable. There is substantial potential for expanded U.S. agricultural products and irrigation technology exports to Morocco.

The U.S. Trade and Development Agency (USTDA) continues to make significant contributions to infrastructure development in Morocco. In 2010 USTDA funded two Reverse Trade Missions to the U.S. in the sectors of renewable energy and ports development. It has also funded a technical assistance for the Agency for Renewable Energy and Energy Efficiency (ADEREE) for the development of 5MW PV solar plant.

As for 2011, USTDA has recently identified projects in several sectors including clean energy, water resources, ports management, and multimodal transports.

In 2007, Morocco and the Millennium Challenge Corporation (MCC) signed a five-year, $697.5 million Millennium Challenge Account Compact to reduce poverty and increase economic growth. The program seeks to stimulate economic growth by improving productivity and increasing employment in high-potential sectors including fruit tree productivity, small-scale fisheries, and handicrafts. Small business creation and growth will also be supported by investments in financial services and enterprise support. The Compact components include:

- Fruit Tree Productivity Project ($300.90 million)
- Small-Scale Fisheries Project ($116.17 million)
- Artisan and Fes Medina Project ($111.87 million)
- Financial Services Project ($46.20 million)
- Enterprise Support Project ($33.85 million)

Market Challenges   Return to top

U.S. exporters face strong competition from European trading partners, particularly France. France and Morocco share a common language and have strong historical ties. European firms in general are familiar with all aspects of Moroccan business culture, financing, regulations and standards. French businessmen also visit Morocco quite often for leisure.

The greatest barriers to trade in Morocco are irregularities and lack of transparency in government procurement procedures, corruption and counterfeit goods. Although the government is diligently working to improve the business environment, foreign corporations still complain about these challenges. The FTA addressed most of these issues and the Moroccan government is striving to make reforms.

The legal and banking systems in Morocco differ in many significant ways from the U.S. systems. The legal system is based on a combination of Spanish, French and Islamic law, making it sometimes complicated for U.S. companies. International and domestic arbitration are accepted and are often used in business contracts. Since the mid 1990s Morocco has made significant reforms to the banking system, focused on structures and programs to attract inbound investment and to facilitate financing of projects and purchases.

Market Opportunities   Return to top

U.S. exporters can benefit from the opportunities opening up through the FTA and take advantage of Morocco's position as a gateway to Europe, Africa and the Middle East.

The U.S. Commercial Service has identified the following sectors as best prospects for U.S. firms. (See Chapter 4)

- Water Management

- Building and Construction
- Renewable Energy
- Safety and security equipment

The following agricultural products are the Foreign Agriculture Service's best prospects. (See Chapter 4)

- Wheat, including durum
- Corn, sorghum, and corn products
- Feed grains and non-grain feed ingredients (in drought years)
- Crude vegetable oil
- Oilseeds and products (soybean meal)

Market Entry Strategy   Return to top

In Morocco, business is based on trust and mutual respect built over time. U.S. exporters will need to travel to Morocco frequently to develop and strengthen relationships in order to do business successfully. U.S. exporters also need to be patient; all procedures take significantly more time to accomplish than U.S. firms may be used to. Moroccans appreciate close working relationships; so working with a locally based agent or distributor will provide U.S. firms with essential knowledge of key contacts, local customs rules and regulations, and niche opportunities. However, market-entry strategies often vary by sector and region. The staff of the U.S. Commercial Service in Morocco is available to provide individualized counseling to determine the best market entry strategy for a given U.S. company/product. U.S. firms are encouraged to contact the U.S. Export Assistance Center for an initial orientation and explanation of export assistance business services.

http://www.buyusa.gov/morocco/en
http://www.export.gov/

Return to table of contents

Return to table of contents

Chapter 2: Political and Economic Environment

For background information on the political and economic environment of the country, please click on the link below to the U.S. Department of State Background Notes.

http://www.state.gov/r/pa/ei/bgn/5431.htm

Return to table of contents

Return to table of contents

Chapter 3: Selling U.S. Products and Services

- Using an Agent or Distributor
- Establishing an Office
- Franchising
- Direct Marketing
- Joint Ventures/Licensing
- Selling to the Government
- Distribution and Sales Channels
- Selling Factors/Techniques
- Electronic Commerce
- Trade Promotion and Advertising
- Pricing
- Sales Service/Customer Support
- Protecting Your Intellectual Property
- Due Diligence
- Local Professional Services
- Web Resources

Using an Agent or Distributor Return to top

Foreign manufacturers and exporters are represented in the market either through branch offices or through authorized agents and distributors. Distributors customarily provide value-added technical support to end-users and often have contractual arrangements under which the local importers provide in-bond warehousing. Although it is legal for a U.S. corporation to be an independent distributor, local agents and distributors are recommended to assist the U.S. firm with know-how and local customs. Some U.S. firms supply Morocco indirectly through regional distribution centers in Europe. Although having regional distribution centers is advantageous in terms of language and shipping, the number of distribution levels makes competitive pricing difficult.

Large-scale stores based on the Costco or Wal-Mart model are a relatively new phenomenon and a good source for direct distribution of consumer products. The Moroccan holding Best Financiere acquired the assets of the German-owned Metro. Metro owned stores in large cities including Casablanca, Rabat, Fes, Tangier and Agadir. The same holding signed a franchise agreement with the French-owned Carrefour.

More traditional European-style supermarkets such as Marjane and Acima are also present in major cities and provide good markets for western food and household supplies. Moroccan supermarkets Label Vie and Aswak Assalam are also present in Casablanca, Rabat, Marrakesh, Tangier and Kenitra and few large DIY hardware stores have opened in Rabat and Casablanca.

The U.S. Commercial Service, co-located with the U.S. Consulate General in Casablanca, provides advice on how to approach the Moroccan market and assists U.S. exporters in their search for potential partners. U.S. companies may also consult their local U.S. Export Assistance Center. For the address and phone number of the nearest U.S. Export Assistance Center, call 1-800-USA-TRADE (1-800-872-8723) or visit www.BuyUSA.gov

Establishing an Office
Return to top

Morocco's 16 Regional Investment Centers are the government's "one stop shops" for the entire registration process, which has been greatly simplified in recent years. The Regional Investment Center is mandated to provide a certificate within one week of providing it a completed application, a passport or ID (or a copy of an ID document if the applicant is not personally present), and 170 dirhams (approx. $20 in February 2011). If the completed certificate is not picked up within one month, it automatically becomes void and one must begin the process again.

Upon receipt of the certificate and after presenting a proof of patent, a registration receipt from the Commerce Registry for 350 dirhams (approx. $42), a fiscal statement and a completed application to the social security savings bank (Caisse Nationale de la Sécurité Sociale), the business can be established. All businesses are subject to inspection by the Regional Investment Centers.

Consult this website for more information on the Regional Investment Centers: http://www.einvest.ma/EInvest%2Di/Cri.aspx#

Franchising
Return to top

Over 400 franchises operate in the fast food, clothing, office supply, furniture, cosmetics, office cleaning and auto repair sectors, representing an increase of 73% over the past three years. Franchise holders are attracted to the marketing image name recognition of well-known U.S. products and brands such as Hertz, McDonald's, Pizza Hut, Dominos Pizza, KFC, Haegen Dazs, TGI Friday's, Papa John's, Budget, New Balance, FutureKids, Century21 and Midas. The successes of franchising stem from an expanding base of young entrepreneurs many of whom are U.S. educated and have the financial means to develop master franchises.

Direct Marketing
Return to top

Marketing services and advertising agencies are increasing their use of direct marketing methods. Common forms in Morocco are point-of-sale promotions, rotating billboards, direct mail and door-to-door sales. Avon and Oriflame (Sweden) are active in door-to-door cosmetic sales.

There is a small but emerging market focused on internet sales and mobile phones. Though small now, this segment may become a major one in the near future, given the growth in the number of young people in Morocco and their tendency to rely on mobile phones and the Internet for information.

Joint Ventures/Licensing   Return to top

Moroccans are increasingly interested in joint venture business opportunities with U.S. partners as a way to modernize Moroccan factories or license technology. As far back as the 1960s, the manufacturing of U.S. products has typically started through joint ventures or acquisition of a local Moroccan firm. Examples are Coca-Cola Export Corp., Procter & Gamble, Colgate Palmolive Maroc, Clark Gum, Fruit of the Loom, Jacob Delafon (Kohler), Johnson & Johnson, Pfizer Laboratories, Pepsi Cola, Simmons Maroc, Kraft Foods and Steelcase

Selling to the Government   Return to top

Moroccan government purchases are handled principally through government tenders and on rare occasions through mutual agreements or private contracts. In the latter case, the government applies directly to firms, which have been traditional suppliers through their representatives in Morocco. Information on government procurement tenders is available in French and Arabic on the following web portal:
http://www.marchespublics.gov.ma/wps/portal

Each ministry issues its own tenders, which are published in newspapers, issuing organizations' websites and announcements distributed to embassies. Deadlines range from 30 to 90 days. Bidding documents are usually published in French and replies must be in French, using French or European standards (i.e., metric, 50/60 htz). The U.S. Commercial Service in Morocco transmits notices of Moroccan government tenders to the U.S. Department of Commerce for listing in the Commerce Business Daily through the Economic Bulletin Board (EBB). Interested U.S. firms can access this information at http://www.export.gov

In 1998, the government approved a decree overhauling the public procurement system to enhance transparency, accountability and competitiveness in procurement. In the last 12 years, Morocco has made significant progress in creating a more transparent tender process. Furthermore, Chapter 9 of the U.S.-Morocco FTA covers national treatment for U.S. firms and transparency and fairness in all transactions. For more information click http://www.ustr.gov/trade-agreements/free-trade-agreements/morocco-fta/final-text

Distribution and Sales Channels   Return to top

Casablanca and Tangier are the primary points of entry for foreign manufactured goods for direct distribution to the public, wholesalers, distributors and retailers. In addition, ferry services between Morocco, Spain and France allow goods to be imported and exported by truck. The $4.3 billion Tanger-Med port with a capacity of 8 million containers is under development and is scheduled for completion by 2015. With its associated free trade zones, it will give Morocco the 15 largest container terminal in the world. The 40-hectare Terminal 1, under a concession to the Danish company APM Terminals, has been operational since June 2007, and Terminal 2, operated by Eurogate

Tanger, opened in August 2008. The port is 35 km east from the northern city of Tangier and is expected to handle merchandise, grain and oil. Additional development is planned for passenger and cruise terminals, roads and train interconnections, and fuel and coal storage facilities.

Selling Factors/Techniques Return to top

Most local distributors of imported merchandise expect their suppliers to provide them with substantial advertising and promotional support, particularly when introducing a new product or brand name. All promotional material and technical documentation should be in French or Arabic depending on the product. Clear and simple French operating instructions are necessary. U.S. firms should train local staff, provide full documentation of products in French, ensure an adequate supply of spare parts, and cooperate in advertising and marketing.

Electronic Commerce Return to top

For more information see Chapter 14 of the U.S.-Morocco FTA at
http://www.ustr.gov/trade-agreements/free-trade-agreements/morocco-fta/final-text

Trade Promotion and Advertising Return to top

Several well known U.S. advertising firms have offices in Morocco that provide services for new product launches, as do several Moroccan advertising agencies, albeit on a smaller scale.

Morocco's literacy rate is 52.3%, giving television a dominant role in the dissemination of information. Television is the most prevalent vehicle for advertising, generating more than 70% of advertising returns. Food, hygiene and beverages are the most common products advertised on television, with multinationals such as Procter & Gamble, Pepsi Cola, and Coca-Cola among the biggest advertisers. Newspapers and periodicals continue to provide advertising space for a variety of products and services, but verification of subscriptions and circulation is difficult. The amount and importance of billboard advertising has dramatically increased in the last few years. Small and medium-sized companies increasingly turn to the Internet as a means of reaching consumers. While the number of Internet users reached 13 million in 2009, the number of internet subscribers is increasing rapidly with a yearly increase of 18% in 2009. Many companies have established web pages, a very economical way to reach a targeted audience.

Pricing Return to top

The market freely determines commodity prices without government involvement with the exception of staple commodities such as gasoline, vegetable oil, sugar, subsidized flour and medicines. In 2003, Morocco implemented a new tariff system for grains (barley, wheat and corn) that resulted in a significant increase in tariffs for bread wheat. The new tariffs supplemented the 1998 system that is still applicable for oilseeds and sugar. Any measure that threatens to raise the price of bread causes great public outcry. As a result, the government managed to raise the price of bread by only 10 centimes in 2004 and has not raised it since.

Sales Service/Customer Support Return to top

It is incumbent upon U.S. firms to supply their local distributor with customer and employee documentation in French. U.S. companies are expected to provide training in brand management and customer support services to their local representatives in order to build strong business rapport and develop product loyalty.

U.S companies should also offer product guarantees and instructions on product care and maintenance in French. As consumers increasingly gain access to low-priced high-quality goods, this information will support the quality level claimed by the supplier.

Morocco lacks the equivalent of a Better Business Bureau and consumer feedback is sometimes difficult to acquire.

Protecting Your Intellectual Property Return to top

The U.S.-Morocco FTA contains some of the strongest intellectual property protection in any free trade agreement. In December 2004, the Moroccan Parliament passed amendments to its existing intellectual property legislation that brought Morocco into compliance with its commitments under the World Trade Organization's Agreement on Trade Related Aspects of Intellectual Property Rights (TRIPS). Morocco has a non-discriminatory legal system that is accessible to foreign investors. The Commercial Courts, established in 1998, have begun to mitigate the weakness in commercial proceedings. A system of commercial arbitration was also created in 1998.

Morocco is a member of the World Intellectual Property Organization (WIPO) and is party to the Bern Copyright, Paris Industrial Property, and Universal Copyright Conventions; the Brussels Satellite Convention; and the Madrid, Nice and Hague Agreements for the Protection of Intellectual Property.

While Moroccan intellectual property laws are generally adequate, enforcement has been an issue. Counterfeiting of clothing, luggage and other consumer goods, as well as the illegal copying of computer software, is common. As a result, many U.S. companies joined together to form their own advocacy group to combat IPR violations. Furthermore, the Business Software Alliance has been successful in educating retailers and consumers regarding software piracy. The Moroccan government is more aggressive when it comes to tackling video piracy, and in response to complaints, the local music community has also stepped up enforcement efforts on CD and audiotape piracy. Canal+, the French satellite subscription service, left Morocco because of the trafficking of pirated de-encryption cards. Counterfeiting of clothing, luggage and even packaged food is increasing at a steady rate. However, as an FTA stipulation, the Moroccan government has promised to crack down on all such activity.

Secured interests in property are recognized and enforced through the "Administration de la Conservation Foncière." The Moroccan government has also passed a law permitting the development of a secondary mortgage market. Furthermore, the Office of Industrial Commercial Property (Office Marocain de la Propriété Industrielle et Commerciale) in Casablanca serves as a registry for intellectual property rights for patents and trademarks in the industrial and commercial sectors. The Moroccan Bureau of Copyrights (Bureau Marocain des Droits d'Auteur) in Rabat registers copyrights for literary and artistic works, including software. Since the FTA went into effect the Moroccan government is using the "first-in-time, first-in-right" principle to honor trademarks and copyrights. In the FTA, the Moroccan government also vows to combat "cyber-squatting" and other digitally related IPR violations. See: http://www.ompic.org.ma. Despite this, the WIPO Internet Treaties have yet to be ratified.

Protecting Your Intellectual Property in Morocco:

Several general principles are important for effective management of intellectual property ("IP") rights in Morocco. First, it is important to have an overall strategy to protect your IP. Second, IP is protected differently in Morocco than in the U.S. Third, rights must be registered and enforced in Morocco, under local laws. Your U.S. trademark and patent registrations will not protect you in Morocco. There is no such thing as an "international copyright" that will automatically protect an author's writings throughout the entire world. Protection against unauthorized use in a particular country depends, basically, on the national laws of that country. However, most countries do offer copyright protection to foreign works under certain conditions, and these conditions have been greatly simplified by international copyright treaties and conventions.

Registration of patents and trademarks is on a first-in-time, first-in-right basis, so you should consider applying for trademark and patent protection even before selling your products or services in the Moroccan market. It is vital that companies understand that intellectual property is primarily a private right and that the US government generally cannot enforce rights for private individuals in Morocco. It is the responsibility of the rights' holders to register, protect, and enforce their rights where relevant, retaining their own counsel and advisors. Companies may wish to seek advice from local attorneys or IP consultants who are experts in Morocco's law. The U.S. Commercial Service can provide a list of local lawyers upon request.

While the U.S. Government stands ready to assist, there is little we can do if the rights holders have not taken these fundamental steps necessary to securing and enforcing their IP in a timely fashion. Moreover, in many countries, rights holders who delay enforcing their rights on a mistaken belief that the USG can provide a political resolution to a legal problem may find that their rights have been eroded or abrogated due to legal doctrines such as statutes of limitations, laches, estoppel, or unreasonable delay in prosecuting a law suit. In no instance should U.S. Government advice be seen as a substitute for the obligation of a rights holder to promptly pursue its case.

It is always advisable to conduct due diligence on potential partners. Negotiate from the position of your partner and give your partner clear incentives to honor the contract. A good partner is an important ally in protecting IP rights. Consider carefully, however, whether to permit your partner to register your IP rights on your behalf. Doing so may create a risk that your partner will list itself as the IP owner and fail to transfer the rights should the partnership end. Keep an eye on your cost structure and reduce the margins (and the incentive) of would-be bad actors. Projects and sales in Morocco require constant attention. Work with legal counsel familiar with Morocco's laws to create a solid contract that includes non-compete clauses, and confidentiality/non-disclosure provisions.

It is also recommended that small and medium-size companies understand the importance of working together with trade associations and organizations to support efforts to protect IP and stop counterfeiting. There are a number of these organizations, both Morocco or U.S.-based. These include:

- The U.S. Chamber and local American Chambers of Commerce
- National Association of Manufacturers (NAM)
- International Intellectual Property Alliance (IIPA)
- International Trademark Association (INTA)
- The Coalition Against Counterfeiting and Piracy
- International Anti-Counterfeiting Coalition (IACC)
- Pharmaceutical Research and Manufacturers of America (PhRMA)
- Biotechnology Industry Organization (BIO)

IP Resources

A wealth of information on protecting IP is freely available to U.S. rights holders. Some excellent resources for companies regarding intellectual property include the following:

- For information about patent, trademark, or copyright issues -- including enforcement issues in the US and other countries -- call the STOP! Hotline: **1-866-999-HALT** or register at **www.StopFakes.gov**.

- For more information about registering trademarks and patents (both in the U.S. as well as in foreign countries), contact the US Patent and Trademark Office (USPTO) at: **1-800-786-9199**.

- For more information about registering for copyright protection in the US, contact the US Copyright Office at: **1-202-707-5959**.

- For more information about how to evaluate, protect, and enforce intellectual property rights and how these rights may be important for businesses, a free online training program is available at www.stopfakes.gov.

- For US small and medium-size companies, the Department of Commerce offers a "SME IP Advisory Program" available through the American Bar Association that provides one hour of free IP legal advice for companies with concerns in Brazil, China, Egypt, India, Russia, and . For details and to register, visit: **http://www.abanet.org/intlaw/intlproj/iprprogram_consultation.html**

- For information on obtaining and enforcing intellectual property rights and market-specific IP Toolkits visit: **www.StopFakes.gov** This site is linked to the USPTO website for registering trademarks and patents (both in the U.S. as well as in foreign countries), the U.S. Customs & Border Protection website to record registered trademarks and copyrighted works (to assist customs in blocking imports of IP-infringing products) and allows you to register for Webinars on protecting IP.

- The U.S. Commerce Department has positioned IP attachés in key markets around the world. You can get contact information for the IP attaché who covers Morocco (located in Egypt) at:
https://www.buyusa.gov/egypt/en/iprtoolkitegypt.html

Due Diligence	Return to top

Potential U.S. investors in Morocco and exporters of U.S goods and service providers are strongly encouraged to perform due diligence and research the bona fides of potential local agents, partners and customers, particularly when extending credit. Due to the absence of a centralized credit agency, U.S. firms, especially those with no previous Morocco experience, should seriously consider the U.S. Department of Commerce International Company Profile (ICP) service prior to signing any agreements with new partners. Using this service, the U.S. exporter can obtain information on the reputation, reliability and financial status of a potential partner in a confidential report, along with a recommendation from the U.S. Commercial Service as to the suitability of the company as a trading partner.

Local Professional Services	Return to top

For information on local professional services providers consult:

- The U.S.-Morocco Chamber of Commerce: http://www.amcham-morocco.com/amcham2011/

- The U.S. Commercial Service Business Service Provider list:
http://www.buyusa.gov/morocco/en/business_service_providers.html

Web Resources	Return to top

http://www.buyusa.gov/morocco/en/

Return to table of contents

Return to table of contents

Chapter 4: Leading Sectors for U.S. Export and Investment

Commercial Sectors

- Renewable Energy
- Building & Construction
- Safety & Security Equipment
- Water Management

Agricultural Sectors

Electricity Generation (GWh generated)	2008	2009	2020
Thermal	5,758	4,850	4,500
Wind	297	390	7200
Hydraulic (net)	785	2,448	1572
Total Renewable Electrical Capacity (GWh/year)	6,840	7,688	13,272
Net Electrical Capacity (GWh/year)	24,002	25,016	61.000

Data Sources: Moroccan Ministry of Energy, Mining, Water and Environment

Because it lacks its own resources of hydrocarbons, Morocco is heavily dependent on fuel imports. As a result, the government recently built on different strategic advantages to elaborate a new vision for its energy market development: proximity to Europe with an existing power connection through Spain and being an active member of the Mediterranean Union. The union's 6 major projects include the Mediterranean solar plan. The goal of this project is to turn the Southern Mediterranean countries into producers of solar energy and then circulating the resulting electricity through the Euro-Mediterranean region. The long term strategy will allow Morocco to become an exporter of green energy as well as a green technology development platform in the MENA region. The energy trading dynamics are also called to change as private high energy consumers will be investing in renewable auto-production.

Morocco is the only North African country with no known substantial fossil fuel deposits. As Morocco's energy supply depends heavily on imports (97%), in 2009 the Moroccan government adopted a strategy based on an accelerated development of its renewable resources. The energy plan expects to increase the renewable share of installed capacity in electricity generation to 42% by 2020 as opposed to 30% in 2009 (of which 24% is from hydroelectric plants).

Morocco's geography and topography provide abundant renewable energy resources:

- Wind resources at a speed reaching 10m/s capable of generating as much as 25GW (Morocco Wind Atlas, CDER, 2007).
- Solar captivity up to 5.7 kwh/m2/day and 3000 hours of sunshine yearly.
- Biomass resources can produce more than 950 MW.

Morocco's electric power production is insufficient to meet a demand that has been increasing at an average annual rate of 8% for the past five years. In 2008, Morocco had an installed capacity from renewable energy of 1.903 GW, of which 90% is large-scale hydroelectric plants. Of the remainder, 82% is wind parks, 12% thermo-solar plants, 5% photovoltaic solar installations and the rest micro-hydroelectric plants and biomass treatment plants. By the end of 2010, this renewable energy installed capacity will increase by 950 MW thanks to the completion of several projects (Tanafnit El Borj hydroelectric, 40 MW; Aïn Beni Mathar thermo-solar plant, 452 MW of natural gas combined cycle and 20 MW of solar; Tangier wind park, 140 MW, Tarfaya wind park, 300MW).

Morocco has a well defined energy strategy for 2009-2020 that aims at to 1) improve security of supply through a more diverse energy mix, 2) increase access to electricity with more competitive pricing, and 3) promote regional integration through increased openness to Euro-Mediterranean power markets. These objectives are supported by two new institutions, the Agency for Development of Renewable Energy and Energy Efficiency (ADEREE) and the Moroccan Agency for Solar Energy (MASEN), and by a $1 billion Fund for Energy Development.

L'Office National de l'Electricité (ONE), a state owned company, is the principal entity in Morocco's electricity sector, with a monopoly on transmission and the largest in-country distribution grid. Unlike transmission activity, power generation in Morocco has been extended to private companies since 1990. Today, IPPs are responsible for approximately half of power production in Morocco. Therefore, IPP developers are the key buyers of equipment. However, ONE remains the sole buyer of electricity production as well as the entity to which IPP assets are transferred after the end of the concession period.

Sub-Sector Best Prospects   Return to top

All power production projects in Morocco are conducted through international tenders for development under a concession basis. U.S. manufacturers of solar/wind/biomass equipment are encouraged to partner with U.S. developers, in order to participate in tenders as joint consortiums.

Also, specialized engineering services are sourced internationally. U.S. companies are encouraged to respond to requests for proposals regarding consultants for the design of technical specifications of large project tenders. Companies should be aware that if they are involved in design tenders they will be prohibited from bidding for subsequent building and management tenders for that particular project.

More than 24,700 jobs are to be created by renewable energy projects by 2030. As such, technical training services for facilities repair and maintenance is part of the government's action plan. Technopolis campus, an industrial park in Rabat, has announced a program dedicated to attracting renewable energy research and development into its facilities.

Opportunities   Return to top

Electricity demand in Morocco is expected to grow by 8.5 % to 9% annually until 2020. This is mainly driven by an ambitious rural electrification plan for 100% coverage. In order to increase the renewable share in its power production, Morocco will be undertaking the following projects:

The Solar Plan Initiative: Launched in 2009, this $9 billion initiative includes the installation of 2000 MW in 5 sites of 10,000 hectares by 2020. A prequalification tender for the phase I (150 MW of Concentrated Solar Power) of the Ouarzazate site (500 MW) was issued in September 2010. A short list of consortiums was announced in December 2010. The listed companies will be invited to bid on a final international tender, involving parabolic trough collector's technology. The plant delivery is slated for 2015.

Other prequalification tenders for consecutive phases are expected before the end of 2012 for different utility scale solar plants technologies, including one with photo-voltaic technology and one with solar tower technology. The short term objective is to have 500MW of solar power operational by 2015. Once the Solar Plan is completed, the solar production will meet 14% of local power demand.

The Moroccan Agency for Solar Energy (MASEN) was created in 2010, and will be responsible for this project. Its mandate is to implement the overall project (design, choice of operators, implementation, and management) and to coordinate and supervise other activities related to this initiative. Stakeholders of the Agency include the Hassan II Fund For Economic & Social Development, Energetic Investment Company and the Office National de l'Electricité, all government entities. More information on the Solar Energy Initiative can be found on: http://www.mem.gov.ma/Ministre/sommaire1.htm.

The EnergiPro program is a set of incentives to encourage private operators to contribute to a total installation of 2000 MW of wind energy by 2010. The Moroccan government encourages private producers of wind power to engage in a tri-party agreement with a Moroccan buyer and the Office National d'Electricite (ONE), which secures the transportation of electric power as well as the purchase of any excess production. This program also involves heavy manufacturers who may choose to produce their own electricity needs. Several private companies, who are major energy consumers, have initiated their own wind parks. For example, Nareva, a subsidiary of Omnium Nord Africain (ONA), the largest private holding in Morocco, is the developer/operator of small scale wind farms. Nareva has signed two agreements recently for the development of two wind parks with the Moroccan rail authority (ONCF) and the Moroccan Airports authority (ONDA).
Furthermore, ONE will take charge for the development of 1000 MW of wind energy by 2020. It has identified 5 sites. The first prequalification tender was issued in November 2010 for the Taza 150 MW site and received 26 participations.

Biomass has the potential of 950 MW based on abundant agricultural resources, including wide areas for livestock breading (2.6 million cattle, 16.3 million sheep and 5.3 million goats). The recent Green Morocco strategy to boost agricultural production and new regulations for waste management represent an additional potential of 400 MW by the year 2030. A U.S. consortium (GESI-Edgeboro-SADAT) won a government tender for the management of the first controlled landfill in Fes in 2002. Today, it is projecting to convert methane gas from the landfill into electricity to power all Fes public lighting.

The Moroccan government requires all its agencies to design an energy efficiency strategy. As such, the construction sector is encouraged to integrate solar resources in building projects (use of solar water heaters).

Morocco's power interconnections, its integration within the EU energy space, and improved green energy price competitiveness will allow it to tap into the European markets for exports of renewable energy.

Moroccan Ministry of Energy, Mining, Water and Environment: www.mem.gov.ma

Office National de l'Electricité: www.one.org.ma

Moroccan Agency for Solar Energy (MASEN): http://www.masen.org.ma/

The building and construction sector continuously contributes 4.5% of the GDP and ranks second in the country's foreign investments. In 2009, the construction sector represented a $33.5 billion market. Government infrastructure projects such as highway and road construction, harbour and airport extensions, private tourism projects, construction of new schools and hospitals, low-cost housing and resorts that combine conference facilities, villas and hotels, all contribute to the building and construction sector growth.

To reach its objective of becoming an international hub and also meet the domestic demand for infrastructure, the Moroccan government plans to invest, by 2015, more than $15 billion to upgrade its basic infrastructure of roads, ports and airports. The demand for transportation services increases at an annual rate of 7-8%. In 2010, the semi private company, Autoroutes du Maroc (ADM), in charge of highway development, completed the construction of approximately 750 miles of highway to connect major Moroccan cities. In 2011 alone, the Moroccan Ministry of Equipment and Transportation will invest $1.7 billion to develop the road infrastructure, including highway systems in the regions of Rabat, Tit Mellil and El Jadida-Safi.

Morocco continues to upgrade its railways system to offer modern trade routes to passengers and goods throughout Morocco. The National Office for Railways (Office National des Chemins de Fer "ONCF") operates 100 trains per day and estimated that the transport of passengers reached 30 million passengers in 2010. Morocco recently signed a $2.4 billion contract with the French firm Alstom for the first phase of a high speed train system, which will include infrastructure, equipment and trains, and connect Casablanca to Tangier by 2015. Additional segment will be opened for bid in the next two-three years. By 2030, ONCF will issue tenders to connect, in less than 4 hours, Tangier to Agadir via Rabat, Casablanca, Marrakech and Essaouira, then Casablanca to Oujda via Meknes and Fez.

In large cities, municipalities are constructing tramways to meet their daily urban transport requirements and curb the use of cars and buses that pollute the environment. In 2007, two tramway lines between Rabat and Sale ($450 million) were started and will transport 400,000 people by the end of 2010. Several extensions to these first two lines are in the planning stages. In 2010, Casablanca started an 18-mile tramway line to be operational in 2012. This project will cost a total of $760 million and is to be financed with $142 million from the municipal budget and loans for the remaining portion. Casablanca has longer term plans for 48 miles to link Casablanca, its suburbs and a 13-mile metro line. These projects will be awarded through international tenders. Other large cities, such as Agadir, Fez, Marrakesh and Tangier also plan to build light metro lines and trams.

With an urban population growth of 4% per year, a need to decongest urban areas and meet the demand for property, the government began a New Cities program aimed at creating 15 new cities by 2020. Under the New Cities program, the government provides land to the public at competitive prices and tax incentives to developers who commit to build 500 low-cost units within five years. To help Moroccans access property, the government established three funds that grant loans at advantageous rates to government employees (Fogaloge-Public Fund), to teachers (Mohammed VI/FOGALEF Fund) and to low-income or temporarily employed people (FOGARIM Fund). Two new cities started in 2004, Tamansourt near Marrakesh, and Tamesna, near Rabat, will provide 88,000 and 54,000 units, respectively, for a total investment of $7.2 billion.

In 2009, the government launched the construction of Ch'rafate, a new city in Tangier, which will provide 30,000 housing units for an investment of $2.9 billion. A further investment of approximately $1.9 billion will build 130,000 low-cost houses priced at approximately $16,887 per unit by 2012. Due to the success of these cities, the government allocated $18 million for studies on additional projects.

Despite the efforts of the government of Morocco to accelerate the production of low cost houses, only 110,000 units are built annually -- not enough to meet demand. To deal with the housing shortage by 2014, Morocco needs to build approximately 158,500 units annually.

To meet demand in the education sector, the Ministry of Education, under its 2009-2012 Emergency Plan began to build 4,774 new schools and extend 187 existing schools. To encourage construction of private schools, Morocco also established the "Fonds de Promotion de l'Enseignement Privé (FOPEP) to co-finance the construction of private schools. The private sector is also negotiating with the Indiana State University to build an American university in Casablanca.

Morocco has very aggressive plans in the tourism sector. It aims to make the country a leading destination, which requires the construction of new facilities, as well as renovation and equipping of existing facilities in order to meet international standards. The Moroccan Government is also implanting "Green Building". In 2008, Morocco created, under its "Green Morocco" program, a special agency, Marchica Med, to develop the lagoon of Marchica, located in the north of Morocco, near Nador. The Marchica lagoon project is located on 10,000 acres and is estimated at $4.6 billion. The investment will cover the construction of "Atalayoun City", an international resort using wind and solar energy, 650 residential villas, a 370-room hotel, 2,230 apartments, a golf academy, sports and leisure infrastructure, two marinas and shops. Marchica Med is slated for completion in 2014, and will be followed by the construction of the Sea City (Cité des Mers) on 37 acres, which will include hotels, 320 villas, 193 apartments and two marinas. In 2015-2020, the Moroccan Government plans to develop the Flamenco Bay (Baie des Flamands) and build, on 190 acres, marinas, golf and resorts.

Sub-Sector Best Prospects   Return to top

Although there is significant competition in the Moroccan building and construction sector, U.S. firms will find excellent opportunities to provide building methods that guarantee safety, and provide short delays in delivery at a lower cost. Currently, Moroccan traditional building methods result in long delays and consequently higher costs, hampering access to property for mid-range income families. U.S. building methods that provide housing at affordable prices have a market with the middle and high-income households. In the tourism sector, U.S. firms will find substantial opportunities to participate in turnkey projects that meet international standards, including a wide range of luxury hotels and resort facilities.

Morocco offers excellent opportunities to U.S. firms in the following segments:

Building materials:
• Innovative building materials
• Steel
• Prefabricated building
• Glass
• Aluminum doors, windows and frame
• Luxury bath tubs, washbasins, and toilet seats
• Luxury bath and kitchen hardware and accessories
• Luxury door and window knobs and fixtures
• Pigments
• Paints, varnishes
• Vinyl floor covering
• Solar water heaters
• Heating/Air conditioning

Equipment:
• Bulldozers and angle dozers
• Rock drilling and earth boring equipment
• Integral tractor shovel loaders
• Shovels, excavators
• Sorting, screening, separating and washing machines for earth, stone, ores, or other mineral substances in solid form
• Crushing machines for earth, stone, ores, etc.
• Grinding machines for earth, stones, etc.
• Concrete/Mortar mixers
• Machines for mixing mineral substances with bitumen
• Escalators and moving walkways

Services:
• Architecture and design

Ministry of Housing: http://www.mhu.gov.ma

Federation of Builders: http://www.fnbtp.ma, http://www.fnpi.co.ma/

International Building and Public Works Trade Show (Salon international du Bâtiment et des travaux publics), November 21-25, 2012, Casablanca http://www.sib.ma/

Safety & Security Equipment

Overview Return to top

Safety and security grew in importance in all key industry sectors in Morocco as a result of increased security incidents and concerns in recent years.

The market for equipment and services, which was negligible a few years ago, is expected to increase by 20% in the next five years. As local production is nonexistent, imported safety and security products supply nearly 95% of the entire market.

Until recently, European firms have dominated the market and have taken advantage of opportunities to provide equipment and services. The competitiveness of U.S. imports is enhanced in part by reduced or zero customs duties (derived from the U.S.-Morocco Free Trade Agreement) and by a low dollar value compared to the Euro.

Moroccan airports, seaports, border crossings, buildings and national security agencies have started upgrading their security systems. In addition, agreements with the United States and other countries require upgrades at airports and seaports.

Morocco's geographic location as a gateway to Europe also requires the protection of borders and checkpoints against illegal immigration, human trafficking and narcotics.

Sub-Sector Best Prospects Return to top

Best prospects include all security and safety equipment and related solutions for seaports, airports, border crossings, security and safety agencies such as the police, and buildings.

Opportunities Return to top

The growing Moroccan safety and security market presents tremendous opportunities for products such as metal detectors, personal access checking systems, walk-through scanners, monitoring and surveillance systems, intrusion detection systems, motion sensors, video cameras, fire prevention and control equipment, alarm equipment for building safety, emergency evacuation systems, radio communication systems, training and services for security equipment, airport specific equipment such as luggage screening devices, biometric systems for access control to secure areas at airports and harbors, and non-intrusive inspection equipment for containers, seaport cargo, etc.

In 2007, Morocco signed an open-skies agreement with the EU. By integrating Morocco's flights with European airspace, Morocco becomes a platform for African countries that do not offer direct flights to Europe, the United States and the Middle East. Morocco also agreed to implement a new system based on satellite and digital technologies (CNS/ATM).

Under its 2008-2012 Development Plan, the Office National des Aéroports (ONDA) (National Airport Authority) will continue to develop new and expand existing airport capacity. In 2009, ONDA invested approximately $179 million in the extension of airports, $36 million in air navigation equipment and $87 in safety and security equipment. During the 2010-2012 years of its Development Plan, ONDA will invest approximately $580 million to expand and equip the existing airports with the following systems:

- fences
- cameras
- luggage screening
- passenger and cargo screening
- radar extension
- radio navigation
- radio communication
- telecommunications
- fire-fighting systems

Moroccan ports handle more than 95% of Morocco's foreign trade. Among the 33 ports under the supervision of the regulator, Agence Nationale des Ports (ANP) and operated by the semi public company Société d'Exploitation des Ports (SODEP, also called Marsa Maroc), Casablanca port is one of the largest in Africa and handles more than 38% of the country's overall imported and exported goods.

To benefit from its strategic geographical location as a gateway to Europe and Africa and become an international logistic platform, the Moroccan government initiated major reforms to improve the competitiveness of its ports. These reforms continue to create opportunities for U.S. suppliers as the Moroccan ports are brought into the international sphere of regulations and agreements. The Moroccan Government, through the ANP, will invest approximately $355 million in 2011-2015 to upgrade the ports infrastructure along its expansive Atlantic coastline. ANP has begun the construction of a third container port in Casablanca. In 2011-2012, ANP will launch the construction of a new port in Safi that will be used to import coal for the National Office of Electricity's thermal station, scheduled to open in 2014, and extend the terminals in Agadir and Nador. ANP will allocate 20% of the total budget to procure the following equipment:

- VTS for the 4 ports of Casablanca, Agadir, El Hoceima and Nador, by the end of 2011
- Container scanner for the port of Casablanca, by 2011
- Video surveillance
- Access control
- Related information systems
- Terminal operating systems

In 2009, the U.S. Trade and Development Agency (USTDA) awarded a $280,238 grant to the National Ports Agency of Morocco (Agence Nationale des Ports, or "ANP"), to conduct a feasibility study for the implementation of a vessel traffic management system and a security/surveillance system (VTMS/security system) at the Casablanca and Safi ports. This grant is expected to lead to international tenders for safety and security equipment. ANP plans to invest approximately $11.5 million to equip:

- Casablanca port with access control and badges
- Safi, Laayoune and Dakhla ports with VTS systems

- Agadir port with a container scanner
- Nador, Al Hoceima, Casablanca, Jorf Lasfar, Agadir and Laayoune ports with passenger and luggage scanners and explosive and narcotics detectors

In 2008, Morocco began construction of a third container terminal in Casablanca. This project will require an estimated 208 million in new safety and security equipment. In 2011, ANP also plans to create a dry port and logistic zone in the area of Casablanca, which will need safety and security equipment for the new hangars and the logistics, and stocking containers.

In 2007, the government completed construction of the first container terminal at Tanger-Med, located in Tangier, now the third largest container port in Africa. The Tanger-Med Special Agency (TMSA) is a semi-governmental Moroccan entity that manages administration of the port's concessions. In 2007, TMSA awarded European-based EADS a contract to provide an integrated maritime security system. Tanger-Med Port is expanding its capacity through a second larger container port, started in 2008. Tanger-Med plans to invest approximately $4.2 billion in safety and security equipment by 2016. Direct shipment from the U.S. to Tanger-Med currently runs from Houston, Mobile, Jacksonville, Charleston and Savannah.

Morocco agreed in 2004 to comply with the International Ship and Port Security Code (ISPS). In order to ship directly to the U.S., Morocco should also comply with the U.S. Maritime Transportation Security Act (MTSA) and the Customs Trade Partnership Against Terrorism (C-TPAT).

In addition to the maritime transportation of goods, a significant number of Moroccan residents abroad enter Morocco through the Port of Tangier. Frequent ferries transport passengers and vehicles between Spain and Morocco. Morocco has several programs underway to encourage a significantly higher number of tourists, up to 10 million by 2010, and the port will need to acquire new equipment such as luggage screening systems, metal detectors, x-ray scanners, access control equipment and fire-fighting systems.

Public and private facilities have begun to acquire security equipment and hire security service companies to protect their staff and buildings against terrorist attacks. Moroccan exporters that target the U.S. market will need to secure their facilities to obtain C-TPAT certification. Also, the demographic growth, unemployment and rural exodus to the major cities contribute to security concerns. In addition, to enhance domestic and border security, and to comply with international regulations, the Ministry of Interior and numerous government agencies, as well as private industries, continue to invest in security equipment. U.S. firms specializing in safety and security will have excellent opportunities in Morocco to sell first-class equipment.

Web Resources   Return to top

Ministry of Equipment and Transport: http://www.mtpnet.gov.ma

Customs Office: http://www.douane.gov.ma

Overseas Security Advisory Council: https://www.osac.gov/Pages/Home.aspx

Tanger-Med Special Agency: http://www.tmsa.ma

Société d'Exploitation des Ports (SODEP also known as MARSA Maroc):
http://www.sodep.co.ma/

Water Management

Overview Return to top

Water supply in the urban area is quasi-universal while in rural areas, access to potable water has reached more than 90% in 2010, compared to 14% in 1995. The less developed area of urban sanitation faces challenges as only 70% of the urban population is connected to sewage systems. It is estimated that urban wastewater will increase from 600 million m3 in 2005, to 900 million m3 in 2020. Currently, wastewater is either discharged into the ocean with only physical treatment or is concentrated in regional basins.

Morocco has developed several models for water management through the construction of dams, large reservoirs and water transfers. Though not yet fully implemented, Law 10-95 of 1995 allows for the establishment of river basin agencies to protect water resources, measures to promote water use efficiency, better allocation of water resources and protection of water quality through the application of user-pays and polluter-pays principles.

To meet expected demand growth for waste water management, Morocco launched the National Sanitation Program (NSP) in 2006. The Program's objective is to develop and improve wastewater collection and reuse to 60% and increase the rate of sanitation access to 80% in urban areas. The Program will cover 10 million people in 260 cities and towns by the year 2020, at an estimated cost of $5.5 billion.

The Prime Minister announced that a total of 79 wastewater treatment plants will be carried out by 2012, worth over $3 billion.

Several governmental agencies have roles in the Moroccan water sector. Major entities include:

The Office National de l'Eau Potable (ONEP) is the main operator in Morocco in the area of water and sanitation. ONEP is responsible for the production of drinking water as it produces 860 million m3 which represents 83% of the nation's potable water. They are also responsible for quality management and water supply transmission to the local agencies. ONEP also contributes in wastewater collection and treatment and the management of sanitation services. ONEP, which has been assigned since 2000 a global ambitious objective by the Moroccan government to manage the sanitation service, now, manages sewerage and wastewater treatment, on behalf of the municipalities to which it supplies drinking water in 72 towns. For a list of tenders in different regions of the country related to water sanitation and potable water, U.S. companies can consult ONEP's website: http://www.onep.ma/AO/

The Ministry of Interior ensures the provision of technical assistance and implementation of infrastructure, control, and application of the drainage policy.

The Ministry of Agriculture and Maritime Fishing is responsible for policy concerning the reuse of wastewater in agriculture.

The Secretariat of State in Charge of Water and Environment is responsible for environmental policy.

Basin Agencies ("Régies") are located in different regions of Morocco and are in charge of evaluating, planning, and managing water resources at the hydraulic basin level. These agencies have authorization for defining conditions required for using treated wastewater.

A Commune Rurale (CR) is responsible for planning, organizing and managing public services, including water supply and sanitation, within their jurisdiction. CRs have the option to provide public services directly, or though a Régie, ONEP, a private operator, or a water user association (WUA).

Sub-Sector Best Prospects   Return to top

Plans for increasing water supply capacity in Morocco offer a growing market to U.S. suppliers of water and wastewater equipment. Morocco needs state-of-the-art technology adapted to new water purification and wastewater treatment equipment.

Water and wastewater treatment projects, rural water distribution technology and desalination projects should be of interest to U.S. firms. The best prospects are: high-pressure water pumps, monitoring equipment, demineralization systems, water treatment and distribution equipment, chemicals for water treatment, and remote control equipment.

Opportunities   Return to top

The African Development Bank and the World Bank are financing several projects for water supply, sanitation and flood protection. For more information U.S companies can visit the following websites:

http://www.afdb.org/en/countries/north-africa/morocco/

http://web.worldbank.org/external/default/main?menuPK=294571&pagePK=141155&piPK=141124&theSitePK=294540

There are many on-going projects in the water sector which offer good opportunities for U.S. suppliers with the several governmental agencies.

ONEP has set ambitious programs and large scale projects to realize its objectives of securing existing urban facilities, generalizing potable water access in rural areas and affording liquid waste sanitation. These projects include:

Rural supply: The objective for ONEP, for the next 5 years, is to bring rural water supply access rate to 95% by the year 2015, by securing facilities and launching individual connections programme and intervening in more than 85 new rural centres.

<u>Urban Supply:</u> For the next 5 years, ONEP projects to improve the distribution network and rehabilitate production, transport and distribution facilities.

The Secretariat of State in Charge of Environment is expected to launch projects over the next 19 years under the 2010 National Strategy for the Development of the Water Sector. However, short, medium and long term projects are not defined yet. Major areas are expected to include:

<u>Water demand management and valuation</u>

- In agriculture, conversion to modern irrigation systems and improvement of existing systems with a potential to save 2.4 billion m3 per year.

- In tourism, developing norms and incentives to use water efficient devices: pipes, water-closets, etc. This is in addition to the improvement of the efficiency of urban water supply networks with a potential to save 120 million m3 per year.

<u>Supply management and development</u>

- Construction of 50 large (3 large dams per year) and 1000 small and mid-sized dams by 2030.

- A North-South transfer at the Bouregreg, Oum Er Rbia and Tensift basins: 800 million m3 per year.

- Rainwater capture pilot projects which could lead to larger-scale deployment similar to what has been done in India and Australia.

- Extension of artificial cloud insemination where possible.

- Desalinization of seawater and demineralization of brackish waters: 400 million m3 per year.

- Reuse of treated wastewater in golf courses, green spaces and crop irrigation: 300 million m3 per year.

<u>Preservation and protection of water resources, natural environment and sensitive areas</u>

- Accelerating the pace of the National Plan for Sanitation and treatment of wastewaters, targeted at an access rate of 90% in 2030.

- A National Sanitation Plan for Rural Areas targeted at an access rate of 90% in 2030.

- A National Plan for the Prevention and Fight Against Industrial Pollution.

- Implementation of the National Plan for the Management of Household and Similar Waste.

- A project to de-mineralize brackish waters for reuse in irrigation and drinking water.

- A five-year project to artificially recharge aquifers.

Web Resources Return to top

The Office National de l'Eau Potable (ONEP): http://www.onep.org.ma

Agricultural Sectors Return to top

The agricultural sector provides an important contribution to the Moroccan economy, accounting for about 15-19% of the GDP and employing almost 40% of the population. Morocco's agricultural production depends mainly on rainfall, as only about 15% of the planted area is irrigated. As a result, agricultural output fluctuates heavily from year to year. With its significant contribution to the country's GDP, the agriculture sector largely determines the growth of the whole Moroccan economy. The large fluctuations in output are also reflected in fluctuations in agricultural imports of some commodities such as animal feed, wheat and oilseeds.

In April 2008, the Moroccan government announced a new strategy for agricultural development that aims at encouraging domestic and foreign investment in agriculture as a mean to generate employment, transfer new technologies and achieve a better integration with the world economy. Major areas for investment have been olives, citrus, grapevines, dairy, exotic fruits, etc. The new strategy also aims at providing leverage for small farmers to consolidate outputs and increase value-added production.

Moroccan agriculture remains mostly traditional with limited applications of production inputs such as fertilizers, pesticides and mechanization. However, many of the export-oriented farms, especially fruits and vegetables, have made a great deal of investment in modern irrigation equipment, new production and marketing technologies that help them meet international standards. Morocco agricultural exports consist mostly of fresh citrus, fruits and vegetables mostly targeted at nearby European markets. In recent years, Morocco's exports to European Union (EU) Markets accounted for about two-thirds of its total agricultural and food exports, which range between $2.0 billion - $2.5 billion. Moroccan exports of agricultural and food products to the United States are relatively small, $100-120 million annually, and consist mostly of olives, olive oil, anchovies, sardines and Clementine.

Morocco imports over $4.0 billion worth of food and agricultural products annually. EU exporters generally supply more than one-third of Moroccan agricultural and food imports, while the U.S. typically provides about 10%-14%. U.S. exports are mostly bulk commodities. However, following the implementation of the U.S.-Morocco Free Trade Agreement (FTA) in January 2006, U.S. exporters increased their market shares of many traditional commodities and gain access to some new-to-market products. The implementation of the FTA boosted the demand for many U.S. high-value agricultural products, such as apples, dried fruits, milk powder, and cheese. More detailed information on the FTA provisions can be found at: www.ustr.gov.

According to official U.S. trade data, U.S. agricultural and food exports to Morocco soared in 2010, compared to 2009. During the period January-October 2010, U.S. agricultural and food products to Morocco rose to $631 million, a 73% increase in U.S. exports of these products during the same period of 2009. Morocco's demand for U.S. bulk commodities are expected to grow in the coming year though at slower pace.

Moroccan Agricultural Imports from the United States (USD Thousands)

Product	2008	2009	Jan - Oct 2009	Jan - Oct 2010	P/P % Change
Bulk Total	**198,722**	**213,348**	**178,741**	**215,279**	**20%**
Wheat	59,886	27,727	16,489	74,815	354%
Coarse Grains	83,881	123,008	113,402	58,307	-49%
Soybeans	46,494	42,574	32,041	53,103	66%
Cotton	7,796	19,335	16,202	28,125	74%
Other Bulk Commodities	424	597	607	929	53%
Intermediate Total	**239,401**	**259,946**	**164,640**	**354,081**	**115%**
Soybean Oil	122,036	140,281	82,282	166,011	102%
Soybean Meal	54,305	76,285	52,846	134,392	154%
Vegetable Oils (Ex Soybean)	577	3,282	852	5,798	581%
Feeds & Fodders	37,618	25,831	19,602	32,997	68%
Live Animals (Dairy Cattle)	6,781	302	290	366	26%
Animal Fats	9,043	7,020	4,169	9,833	136%
Planting Seeds	3,317	2,368	1,860	1,957	5%
Other Intermediate Products	5,724	4,577	2,739	2,727	0%
Consumer Oriented Total	**86,037**	**31,490**	**21,432**	**61,119**	**185%**
Dairy Products	77,774	21,767	13,582	54,585	302%
Fresh Fruit (Apples)	1,724	1,695	1,695	644	-62%
Processed Fruit & Vegetables	353	839	679	2281	236%
Fruit & Vegetable Juices	1,646	875	875	36	-96%
Tree Nuts	3,348	5,603	3,997	2,555	-36%
Other Consumer Oriented	1,192	711	604	1,018	69%
Forest Products	**940**	**958**	**827**	**948**	**15%**
Fish Products	**164**	**73**	**73**	**8**	**-89%**
Grand Total	**525,264**	**505,815**	**365,713**	**631,435**	**73%**

Source: Department of Commerce, U.S. Census Bureau, Foreign Trade Statistics

P/P : Period to Period

Best Prospects for Morocco are:

- Wheat, including durum
- Corn and sorghum for feeding, and corn products
- Feed grains and non-grain feed ingredients (in drought years)
- Crude vegetable oil
- Oilseeds and products (soybean meal)
- Purebred pregnant dairy cattle and dairy semen
- Fattening cattle
- Milk powder, unsalted butter, whey, cheese for pizza
- Dried fruits and nuts (pistachios, walnuts, non-pitted prunes, raisins, and almonds)
- Apples (red and golden delicious)
- Confectionary items
- Seafood/frozen
- Canned products.

Several consumer-oriented food products offer good opportunity for U.S. suppliers in spite of the high freight cost. These include sauces, condiments, canned fruit and vegetables, confectionary and snack foods.

Associations' contacts:

Pure-bred Dairy Cattle Association
(Association Nationale des Eleveurs de Bovins de Races Pures ,ANEB)
M. Zniber Seddik, President
5, Rue Mohamed Triki, Residence Tissir, Im. B. Apt. 2
Rabat 10050, Morocco
Phone: (212-53) 723-0244 Fax: (212-53) 723-0262
Email: aneb@menara.ma

Feed and Poultry Federation
(Fédération Interprofessionnelle du Secteur Avicole, FISA)
Khair-Eddine SOUSSI; President
123, Boulevard Emile Zola
Casablanca 20310, Morocco
Phone: (212-52) 231-1249   Fax: (212-52) 244-2276
Website: www.fisa.org.ma   Email: fisa@iam.net.ma

Cereals and Grains Traders Federation
(Fédération des Négociants de Céréales et Légumineuses, FNCL)
M. Bouchaib EL HADDAJ
57 Avenue Abdelmoumen, Residence El Hadi
Batiment B4, 1er etage, Casablanca, Morocco
Phone: (212-25) 247-6438/247-6468   Fax:(212-25) 247-4207
Email: fncl@wanadoo.net.ma

In country USDA contacts:

Office of Agricultural Affairs, U.S. Embassy Rabat
Dr. Hassan F. AHMED, *Regional Agricultural Attaché*
M. Idriss EL HONSALI, *Agricultural Specialist*
Phone: (212-35) 776-5987   Fax: (212-35) 776-5493
Email: AgRabat@usda.gov

List of USDA/FAS Commodity Reports and Briefs:

In addition to the scheduled reports listed on the table below, the Agricultural Attaché regularly reports on special issues (such as significant changes in policy). Public FAS/USDA agricultural and food reports can be found at http://www.fas.usda.gov/scriptsw/attacherep/default.asp

Report	Expected Date
Grain and Feed Annual	March 15th
Food/Agriculture Import Regulation And Standards (FAIRS)	July 1st
FAIRS Export Certificates	July 15th
AgExporter Guide	September 1st
Citrus Annual	November 15th
Selling Food Products to Retail Sector	December 30th
Selling Food Products to Hotels, Restaurants & Institutional	June 15th

Return to table of contents

Chapter 5: Trade Regulations, Customs and Standards

- Import Tariffs
- Trade Barriers
- Import Requirements and Documentation
- U.S. Export Controls
- Temporary Entry
- Labeling and Marking Requirements
- Prohibited and Restricted Imports
- Customs Regulations and Contact Information
- Standards
- Trade Agreements
- Web Resources

Import Tariffs   Return to top

Under the U.S.-Morocco FTA, tariffs on more than 95% of qualifying consumer and industrial goods were immediately eliminated. Remaining tariffs for most qualifying goods will be eliminated over a nine-year period that began on January 1, 2006. For a limited number of products, tariffs will be eliminated over a period of up to 15 years.

The agreement also offers new access to services, intellectual property protection, a predictable legal framework for U.S. investors, open and fair government procurement, and strong protections for labor and environment.

If the import is an unfinished product requiring further processing or assembly in Morocco, duties may be reduced further. Import duties vary from 2.5 to 35% for many raw materials and equipment. Imports are also subject to a Value Added Tax (VAT), varying from 0 to 20%. VAT is not always paid on locally produced goods (e.g., corn) or on some vehicles used for international transportation (e.g., moving vans).

In addition to the 1995 Finance Act, a para-fiscal tax (taxe parafiscale) of 0.25% on imports was introduced to finance activities such as technical inspections for export goods, economic and export promotion, industrial development, and small-scale production. The following are exempt from the "taxe parafiscale": All merchandise imports qualifying for:

1. Special customs procedures or concessions granted in the context of officially approved investment programs,

2. Exemption or total relief from import duties and taxes by virtue of legislative provisions or special regulations, and

3. Preferential trading agreements between Morocco and other countries.

Non-tariff barriers in Morocco range from language and cultural differences to oligopolies in certain key industrial sectors such as banking, insurance and cement, standards that favor EU brands, and lack of efficient and transparent processes for obtaining government permits, land approvals and government procurements.

The language and cultural differences are subtle and need to be addressed. French is the dominant business language, and business models are often based on traditional French models. Many of Morocco's elite were educated in France and feel at ease with the French models. All government tenders are issued in French and bids must be submitted in French.

Convincing local oligopolies that liberalized trade and investment policies will benefit them in the medium to long term by expanding the business pie has been a challenge. Nevertheless a number of U.S. firms are taking the lead in the tourism and franchising sectors. Other market openings such as in the banking, insurance and cement sectors will require a shift in mentality. In general, competition is not welcomed because the business pie traditionally has been relatively small. Significant new investments, however, are beginning to expand the pie.

A number of forward leaning provisions in the FTA require the Government of Morocco to improve business procedures, reduce corruption and improve transparency in government procurement. The U.S. Embassy and the U.S. Consulate General are monitoring the government's efforts to make improvements.

The following documentation is required for all imports and exports:

1. A license representing the "physical import or export".

2. A commercial invoice: Pro-forma invoices are provided in most cases. No special invoice form is necessary. The commercial or pro-forma invoice should (a) be on the supplier's letterhead, (b) fully describe the goods in French, (c) indicate the HS code when available, (d) indicate the value of the goods, (e) indicate the currency for payment (for foreign exchange transfer), and (f) indicate the address of the buyer. U.S. exporters should keep in mind that the date format should be (dd/mm/yy).

3. An "import commitment"(engagement d'importation), which is the authorization provided by the exchange office for transfer of foreign currencies from Morocco to foreign suppliers abroad.

4. A "customs declaration" (declaration de douane) is provided by the customs office and is required for import and export through a port or airport. For shipments by mail, a simple form filled out at the post office replaces the "declaration de douane."

5. The importer/exporter may attach any documentation, such as technical documentation, that might help the customs office.

The U.S. and Morocco have differing interpretations of transshipments of ships, vis a vis the FTA. The Agreement states:

ARTICLE 5.9: TRANSIT AND TRANSSHIPMENT
For purposes of this Chapter, each Party shall provide that a good shall not be considered to be imported directly from the territory of the other Party if the good undergoes subsequent production, manufacturing, or any other operation outside the territories of the Parties, other than unloading, reloading, or any other operation necessary to preserve it in good condition or to transport the good to the territory of the other Party.

Morocco is current reviewing its policy on transshipment under the FTA. Goods transshipped through a third country port should be accompanied by a bill of lading showing Morocco as the final destination of the goods, and invoices issued by the U.S. company, addressed to the Moroccan importer. In addition, a "certificate of non manipulation" is also required by Moroccan customs.

The documentation required for import or export of digitalized products electronically delivered over the Internet (i.e., software, movies and downloads) or other networks, is the same as the documentation previously listed.

When sending promotional material, and especially promotional videos, it is important to clearly state, in French, "Promotional Use Only" and "No Commercial Value."

U.S. Export Controls   Return to top

The Bureau of Industry and Security (BIS) of the U.S. Department of Commerce is responsible for implementing and enforcing the Export Administration Regulations (EAR), which regulate the export and re-export of most commercial items. It often refers to the items that BIS regulates as "dual-use" – items that have both commercial and military or proliferation applications – but purely commercial items without an obvious military use are also subject to the EAR. For information on Commerce Department export controls click here: http://www.bis.doc.gov/licensing/exportingbasics.htm

Temporary Entry   Return to top

Goods imported under a temporary entry provision must be approved by decree from the Finance Ministry. Customs may authorize entry of goods on an individual basis. The limit for temporary entry is six months, renewable for up to two years.

Labeling and Marking Requirements   Return to top

No special regulations apply to the exterior marking of containers for shipments to Morocco. However, an indication on outer containers of the net weight in kilograms, together with other identification markings, will assist in locating goods on arrival and speed their clearance through customs. Duties and taxes are assessed on the value indicated on the commercial invoice.

Food labels can be in French or Arabic and must show country of origin. Both local and imported canned foods and beverages must have the dates of production and expiration printed on them.

The metric measurement is mandatory. Moroccans are not familiar with U.S. measurements and standards. Metric measurements are common on both local and imported products. Also, unlike in Egypt and other Middle Eastern countries, most Moroccans exclusively use the same numbers (characters) as those used in the U.S. When using the date format (xx/xx/xx), U.S. exporters should keep in mind that the date format should be (dd/mm/yy). The NM 09.000 is the standard required labeling on textile products, and the Agricultural Attaché's office in Rabat has prepared a Food and Agricultural Import Regulations and Standards (FAIRS) report for U.S. exporters detailing agricultural labeling requirements that can be found at http://www.fas.usda.gov/scriptsw/attacherep/default.asp

Prohibited and Restricted Imports	Return to top

Import restrictions apply only to firearms, explosives, used clothing, used tires, pornography, absinthe, kif and rugs similar to those produced in Morocco.

Customs Regulations and Contact Information	Return to top

In the last few years, Moroccan customs has endeavored to streamline its processes. In addition to the last customs survey results indicating high levels of client satisfaction, the American Chamber of Commerce reports that the average waiting time has been reduced to just a few hours.

For more information on import duties for specific products, U.S. exporters should contact the customs office (Direction Generale des Douanes), Avenue Annakhil, Centre des Affaires, Hay Raid, Rabat, Morocco, tel: (212)-537-57-90-00; fax: (212)-537- 71-78-14/15; e-mail: adii@douane.gov.ma. The customs website (http://www.douane.gov.ma) is also a great reference in French for customs-related issues.

Standards	Return to top

- Overview
- Standards Organizations
- Conformity Assessment
- Product Certification
- Accreditation

Overview

The Moroccan Industrial Standardization Office (Service de Normalisation Industrielle Marocaine or "SNIMA") is the Moroccan organization responsible for developing standards. As the unique standardization body in Morocco, it not only provides all product norms and standards certification, but it also is the sole provider of management system certification. It is responsible for answering all questions related to the Technical Barriers to Trade Agreement. Furthermore, this office annually creates a list of consumer and industrial products for which it intends to create norms and standards for the following year. A list of products that will receive updated norms and standards and details concerning the process is available on http://www.snima.ma/ under "Normes en enquête." The national goal is to increase the number of certified product norms by 15 to 20 percent over each of the next three years. With the total number increasing to 5,000 certified product norms in the next three years, domestic and international trade will be facilitated and product quality will be ensured for the Moroccan consumer. SNIMA's long-term strategy also focuses on gaining official recognition from the International Accreditation Forum.

Standards Organizations

Service de Normalisation Industrielle Marocaine (SNIMA)
Angle Avenue Kamal Zebdi et Rue Dadi,
Secteur 21 Hay Riad, Rabat
Tel: (212) 537 71 62 14
Fax: (212) 537 71 17 98
Email: snima@mcinet.gov.ma

The Ministry of Agriculture's inquiry point on standards:
The National office for food safety (Office National de Securité Sanitaire des Produits Alimentaires -ONSSA)
Avenue Hadj Ahmed Cherkaoui, Agdal – Rabat
Tel: (212) 537 67 65 00
Fax: (212) 5 37 68 20 49
Website: www.onssa.gov.ma

La Direction des Contrôles et de la Protection des Végétaux
Contact: Mohamed Belkacimi
E-mail:elbelkacemi.mohamed@gmail.com

La Division de la Réglementation et de la Normalisation;
Contact: Hamid Lachab
E-mail: hamid.lachhab@gmail.com

NIST Notify U.S. Service
Member countries of the World Trade Organization (WTO) are required under the Agreement on Technical Barriers to Trade (TBT Agreement) to report to the WTO all proposed technical regulations that could affect trade with other Member

countries. **Notify U.S.** is a free, web-based e-mail subscription service that offers an opportunity to review and comment on proposed foreign technical regulations that can affect your access to international markets. Register online at Internet URL: http://www.nist.gov/notifyus/

Conformity Assessment   Return to top

The main national testing organization is the Laboratory for Public Tests and Studies (Laboratoire Public d'Essais et d'Etudes or LPEE). LPEE currently has laboratories in all of Morocco's major cities. Although most of its work is dedicated to building and construction testing, it also deals with electrical and calibration testing. SNIMA also created technical industrial centers that will specialize in mechanical, chemical and transportation testing.

Product Certification   Return to top

The following five government commissions have the sole mandate to certify products:
1. Multi-sector Commission (Commission pluri-sectorielle), which includes services,
2. Food and Agricultural Industry Certification Commission (Commission de Certification des Industries Agro-Alimentaires),
3. Chemical and Para-Chemical Industry Certification Commission (Commission de Certificat des Industries de la Chimie et de la Parachimie),
4. Mechanic, Metallurgic, Electric and Electronic Certification Commission (Commission de Certification des Industries Mécaniques, Métallurgiques, Electriques et Electroniques),
 5. Textile and Leather Industry Certification Commission (Commission de Certification des Industries du Textile et du Cuir).

SNIMA conforms to the international guide ISO/IEC 65. Once products conform to this standard, the Ministry of Industry, Commerce and New Technologies will grant the product the right to use the NM label as proof of its quality. All products must also conform to the specifications of the FTA.
http://www.moroccousafta.com/index_ang.htm

Accreditation   Return to top

The only Moroccan accreditation body is the Ministry of Industry, Commerce and New Technologies. Although accreditation is still voluntary with no accreditation requirements required by technical regulations, there are almost 30 certified labs nationwide. A complete list of these labs can be found at the website http://www.mcinet.gov.ma by clicking on "Qualité-Métrologie-Accréditation," then "Accréditation" and finally "Liste des laboratories accrédités."

Trade Agreements   Return to top

The U.S.-Morocco FTA went into effect in 2006. This agreement was the second FTA with an Arab nation and the first on the continent of Africa. This FTA is comprehensive and provides IPR, labor and environment provisions.

Morocco has also agreed to make its business environment far more transparent and welcoming to foreign companies by providing companies with an efficient, legal framework and secure working environment. Both governments have agreed to publish their current trade and investment laws and publish any proposed legislation in advance. Bribery of any form will be outlawed; whistle-blowers will be granted protection, and U.S. companies will enjoy the same rights as Moroccan companies when investing. Furthermore, the Moroccan government has promised to grant U.S. companies the same legal rights that they enjoy in the U.S. system such as effective, impartial legal dispute settlement, including due process protection and transparent public trials. There is also a non-discriminatory clause legally mandating that all U.S. businesses trying to physically invest in Morocco will have equal access to infrastructure such as phone switches and submarine cable landing stations. Trademarks, copyrights, patents and trade secrets will receive the same protection they receive under U.S. law even when in digital form. Intellectual Property Rights will also be protected through the enforcement of tough laws outlawing both piracy and counterfeit products.

This agreement will also work to uphold labor and environmental standards. Neither party can reduce its current standards.

The full text of the agreement along with a main point summary, a trade guide and list of key contacts can be found at http://www.moroccousafta.com/index_ang.htm

Morocco also has FTAs with United Arab Emirates, Jordan, Tunisia, Egypt, Turkey and the EU. These agreements illustrate Morocco's drive to liberalize its business environment by adopting internationally accepted business law, accounting procedures and technical norms in order to foster internationalization and economic development.

The EU-Moroccan Association Agreement went into effect on April 1, 2000 and is equally valid for all U.S. companies located in Morocco. The agreement calls for the gradual elimination of tariffs on EU-Moroccan trade in industrial goods over 12 years and provides duty-free access for limited quantities to some agricultural products, especially seafood products, fruits and vegetables. In October 2008, Morocco gained "advanced status," which will allow both parties to consider a comprehensive free trade agreement.

Web Resources   Return to top

http://www.moroccousafta.com/index_ang.htm

http://www.export.gov/middleeast

Return to table of contents

Chapter 6: Investment Climate

- Openness to Foreign Investment
- Conversion and Transfer Policies
- Expropriation and Compensation
- Dispute Settlement
- Performance Requirements and Incentives
- Right to Private Ownership and Establishment
- Protection of Property Rights
- Transparency of Regulatory System
- Efficient Capital Markets and Portfolio Investment
- Competition from State Owned Enterprises
- Corporate Social Responsibility
- Political Violence
- Corruption
- Bilateral Investment Agreements
- OPIC and Other Investment Insurance Programs
- Labor
- Foreign-Trade Zones/Free Ports
- Foreign Direct Investment Statistics
- Web Resources

Openness to Foreign Investment   Return to top

Morocco actively encourages foreign investment and has sought to facilitate it through macro- economic policies, trade liberalization, and structural reforms. The U.S. Free Trade Agreement (FTA) and the Association Agreement with the EU have led Morocco to reduce its tariffs on imports from the U.S. and EU. Morocco has also signed a quadrilateral FTA with Tunisia, Egypt and Jordan, and a bilateral FTA with Turkey. Additionally, it is seeking trade and investment accords with other African, Asian and Latin American countries.

The U.S.-Morocco FTA has led to a 150% increase in bilateral trade and roughly tripled both the stock and annual flow of U.S. investment to Morocco. Nonetheless, challenges remain. According to the World Bank's 2009 "Doing Business in Morocco" report, the country's excessive bureaucratic red tape continues to be a major constraint on the competitiveness of the economy and deters investors. To facilitate foreign investment, the government has created a number of Regional Investment Centers (CRI) to minimize and accelerate administrative procedures. Investments in excess of 200 million MAD ($26 million) are, in addition, referred to a special ministerial committee chaired by the Prime Minister.

Morocco's 1995 Investment Charter applies to both foreign and Moroccan investors, with foreign exchange provisions favoring foreign investors. Foreign investment is permitted in nearly every sector. The world's largest phosphate producer, Morocco's Office

Cherifien des Phosphates (OCP), has signed several joint venture agreements to set up new fertilizer and chemical plants, a move seen by analysts as a step towards liberalizing the phosphate sector. OCP appears to have shelved previous plans for an initial public offering, however. Additionally, although foreigners are prohibited from owning agricultural land, the law does allow for long-term leases of up to 99 years and permits agricultural land to be purchased for non-agricultural purposes. Morocco has sought to encourage foreign investment in the agricultural sector by making land available for leasing. Agricultural ventures by French, Spanish and Middle Eastern investors are targeted mostly at citrus and olives, with some small investments in grapes and berries.

Year	Index	Ranking
2010	TI Corruption Index	85 out of 178
2010	Heritage Economic Freedom	91 out of 179
2011	World Bank Doing Business	114 out of 183
2011	MCC Gov Effectiveness	68th Percentile
2011	MCC Rule of Law	58th Percentile
2011	MCC Control of Corruption	65th Percentile
2011	MCC Fiscal Policy	74th Percentile
2011	MCC Trade Policy	56th Percentile
2011	MCC Regulatory Quality	74th Percentile
2011	MCC Business Start Up	79th Percentile
2011	MCC Land Rights Access	68th Percentile
2011	MCC Natural Resource Mgmt	20th Percentile

Conversion and Transfer Policies   Return to top

The Moroccan dirham is convertible for foreign investors for all current-account and selected capital-account transactions. Particularly, capital-account repatriation transactions are convertible if the original investment is registered with the foreign exchange office. Morocco's foreign exchange law enables expatriate employees to repatriate their entire salaries.

Foreign exchange is readily available through commercial banks for the following activities without prior government approval: Remittances by foreign residents; repatriation of dividends and capital by foreign investors; and payment for foreign technical assistance, royalties and licenses.

The current exchange-rate regime is a tightly managed float against a euro-dominated basket of currencies. The Moroccan dirham thus tends to move in line with the Euro. It fluctuated between 8 and 9 MAD to the dollar in 2010, with an average exchange rate for the year of 8.42 MAD to the dollar.

Expropriation and Compensation   Return to top

Mission Morocco is not aware of any recent, confirmed instances of private property being expropriated for other than public purposes, or being expropriated in a manner that is discriminatory or not in accordance with established principles of international law.

Dispute Settlement Return to top

In general, investor rights are backed by an impartial procedure for dispute settlement that is transparent. In 2009 a few U.S. companies had investment disputes with the Government of Morocco but no new cases emerged in 2010. In most cases, through U.S. advocacy, these minor disputes were resolved with the relevant government agencies.

While Morocco's commercial and appeals courts have generally improved the dispute settlement climate, Moroccan and foreign companies continue to complain about the inefficiency and the lack of transparency in the judicial system. Among King Mohammed VI's six priority areas identified in a major annual address in August 2009 were improving the business environment and the fairness and efficiency of the judicial system. The King's emphasis is well placed, as recent UN and World Bank studies highlight Morocco's shortcomings in this area, indicating that bankruptcy protection and liquidation procedures are inefficient and that the courts are slow and often fail to enforce legal rulings.

In an effort to promote foreign investment, the Moroccan legislature has adopted laws to protect both foreign investors and their Moroccan counterparts. Morocco is a member of the International Center for the Settlement of Investment Disputes (ICSID) and a party to the 1958 Convention on the Recognition and Enforcement of Foreign Arbitral Awards (with reservations) and the 1965 Convention on the Settlement of Investment Disputes between States and Nationals of Other states. Legislation extending the scope of arbitration and mediation and giving them added legal standing took effect in July 2007, partly as a result of FTA required reforms. Arbitration, in particular, finds increasing use in Morocco today. Moreover, USAID, in collaboration with IFC, assisted the Government in 2008 and 2009 with the establishment of a national commission on Alternative Dispute Resolution (ADR) with a mandate to regulate mediation training centers and develop mediator certification systems. The goal of this program is to increase the use of mediation in the prevention phase of bankruptcy proceedings and in the resolution of business disputes outside of the courts. Although the program remains limited in its implementation, the business community has generally viewed early use of the system in Rabat and Casablanca as favorable.

Performance Requirements and Incentives Return to top

At present, there are no general foreign investor performance requirements. However, in the event that government incentives are provided, requirements may be imposed, and if so, would be spelled out in the specific investment contract.

Morocco provides a range of investment incentives, including a corporate tax holiday during the first five years of business and a 17.5% rate thereafter. In the case of "offshoring" facilities, the government has offered telecommunications costs set at 35% below the market price and training grants of up to $7,000 for each Moroccan employee during the first three years of employment. A new version of the investment incentive regime is currently undergoing a governmental review.

U.S. citizens can enter Morocco for a period of three months without a visa. A Moroccan residence permit is required for a period of more than three months.

Right to Private Ownership and Establishment Return to top

Private ownership is permitted in all but a few sectors reserved for the state, such as phosphate mining. Economic analysts, however, speculate that as Morocco's phosphate processing increasingly becomes open to foreign investment, its mining sector may follow suit. Apart from a few exceptions, private entities may freely establish, acquire and dispose of interests in business enterprises.

In 2009 a number of firms including the national port operator (Marsa Maroc) were placed on the short list of companies to be privatized in the future.

Protection of Property Rights Return to top

The U.S.-Morocco FTA contains strong intellectual property protections, which were incorporated in Moroccan intellectual property legislation in 2006. Pursuant to its FTA obligations, Morocco enacted legislation that increased protection of trademarks, copyrights and patents. While the protection of Intellectual Property Rights (IPR) is improving as a result of these provisions, counterfeit DVDs and CDs remain widely available throughout Morocco and weaknesses remain in country's mechanisms for detection and sanctioning of internet-based IPR violations. Morocco's Customs Office, Copyright Office (BMDA), and the Office of Industrial and Commercial Property (OMPIC) have initiated campaigns to target Morocco's largest counterfeit manufacturers and importers, with mixed success. Consumer product companies have stated that counterfeiters have become increasingly sophisticated in their production and distribution of counterfeit goods.

Secured interests in property are recognized and enforced through the "Administration de la Conservation Foncière."

Transparency of Regulatory System Return to top

Despite government efforts to increase the system's transparency, Morocco's administration is opaque and difficult to navigate. Routine permits, especially those required by local government agencies, can be difficult to obtain. Morocco has sought, with some success, to increase the transparency of its public tenders. However, recent moves to decentralize the procurement process have seen only limited implementation pending the government's general "regionalization" plan.

In 2006 a new charter for the central bank created an independent board of directors and prohibited the Ministry of Finance and Economy from borrowing from the central bank except in exceptional circumstances.

Morocco's banking system is one of the most liberalized in North Africa. Nonetheless, it is highly concentrated, with the six largest banks accounting for 85% of banking sector assets. The IMF/World Bank's updated Financial System Stability Assessment concluded that the system was "stable, adequately capitalized, profitable and resilient to shocks." It noted the progress Morocco has made in deepening financial intermediation (39% of the population has a bank account as of 2009, up from 36% in 2007) and in reducing the overall level of non-performing assets (down from 11% in 2006 to 6% at the end of 2008 and 5.5% by the end of 2009).

A new Moroccan banking law was passed in 2006, strengthening the supervisory power of the central bank and improving risk management practices. Morocco has generally completed adoption of Basel II capital adequacy and risk management guidelines in order to improve financial stability and adopted International Accounting Standards (IAS) intended to enhance transparency.

Credit is allocated on market terms, and foreign investors are able to obtain credit on the local market. There are some cross-shareholding arrangements, but they are not tailored to exclude foreign investment. The Mission has not received any reports of efforts by the private sector or industry to restrict foreign participation in standard-setting organizations. The government has actively sought out the participation of foreign investors for discussions on improving the business climate in Morocco.

Some foreign banks are critical of what they view as a lack of proportional participation in the Moroccan Bankers' Association. However, Moroccan banks are largely in compliance with the Basel I standards and have become almost completely Basel II compliant as required by the Moroccan central bank. Banks are supervised on a consolidated basis and must provide statements audited by certified public accountants. In 2009, ten banks submitted consolidated financial statements based on Basel II standards.

The Casablanca Stock Exchange (CSE), founded in 1929 and re-launched as a private institution in 1993, is one of the few regional exchanges with no restrictions on foreign participation. The market weakened in 2008 and fell further in 2009 when the global credit crisis and its spillover into the real economy dampened foreign investment inflows and demand for exports. The Bourse rebounded sharply in 2010 with the MASI (Moroccan All Shares Index) growing by 21.17%. Although the Casablanca exchange only saw two Initial Public Offerings (IPOs) during 2010, one of the listings came from Morocco's largest and most important insurance company, CNIA SAADA Assurance, which listed 15% of its shares on the exchange in November. Investors predict more listings and similar gains in 2011 as the Bourse focuses on outreach to its African neighbors.

Analysts note that the market is buoyed by continuing restrictions on the ability of Moroccans to invest abroad. Gradual easing of these limits is widening Moroccan investors' options, however, and recent changes in the Moroccan exchange regime seem aimed at allowing Moroccan financiers to invest more freely into neighboring markets.

Competition from State Owned Enterprises Return to top

Morocco maintains partial or full state ownership in several sectors, from phosphate mining to transportation. While the leaders of Morocco's state-owned enterprises (SOE) are appointed by the King, most report to a Board of Directors chaired by a Minister or royal or prime ministerial appointee and publish annual reports.

SOEs compete with private firms under the same terms and conditions.

Corporate Social Responsibility Return to top

CSR has gained strength in tandem with Morocco's economic expansion and stability. The country's businesses are slowly embracing responsibility for the impact of their activities on the environment, communities, employees and consumers. As an example, the General Federation of Moroccan Businesses (CGEM) has awarded "social labels" to companies based on a systematic analysis of the effects of their activities. While there is no legislation mandating specific levels of CSR, foreign and some local enterprises follow generally accepted principles such as the OECD CSR guidelines for multinational companies. NGOs are also taking an increasingly active role in monitoring corporations' CSR performance.

Political Violence Return to top

Morocco is a monarchy with a Constitution, government, parliament and judiciary, in which ultimate power and authority rest with the throne. A democratic reform process is underway and the country is broadly regarded as politically stable. The U.S. Government maintains excellent relations with Morocco and has designated Morocco a Major non-NATO Ally. A series of terrorist bombings in Casablanca in March and April 2007, the first major incidents since the Casablanca bombings of 2003, highlighted the fact that Morocco continues to face a terrorist threat. U.S. facilities were targeted in 2007. Counterterrorism cooperation is excellent. The Moroccan Government aggressively investigates terrorist suspects and has dismantled a number of terrorist cells over the past year.

Demonstrations occur frequently in Morocco and usually center on domestic issues. During periods of heightened regional tension, large demonstrations may take place in major cities. Although these demonstrations have been peaceful, well organized, and well controlled by the police, past events have exhibited anti-U.S. sentiment with isolated violent incidents.

The sparsely settled Western Sahara was the site of armed conflict between the Moroccan Government and the Polisario Front, which demands independence. A cease-fire has been in effect since 1991, but the territory remains disputed between Morocco, Algeria, and the Polisario. Negotiations to reach a settlement resumed in 2007 under UN auspices, but the dispute hampers development in the territory, as well as economic and political integration in the North Africa region.

Corruption, including bribery, raises the costs and risks of doing business. Corruption has a corrosive impact on both market opportunities overseas for U.S. companies and the broader business climate. It also deters international investment, stifles economic growth and development, distorts prices, and undermines the rule of law.

It is important for U.S. companies, irrespective of their size, to assess the business climate in the relevant market in which they will be operating or investing, and to have an effective compliance program or measures to prevent and detect corruption, including foreign bribery. U.S. individuals and firms operating or investing in foreign markets should take the time to become familiar with the relevant anticorruption laws of both the foreign country and the United States in order to properly comply with them, and where appropriate, they should seek the advice of legal counsel.

The U.S. Government seeks to level the global playing field for U.S. businesses by encouraging other countries to take steps to criminalize their own companies' acts of corruption, including bribery of foreign public officials, by requiring them to uphold their obligations under relevant international conventions. A U. S. firm that believes a competitor is seeking to use bribery of a foreign public official to secure a contract should bring this to the attention of appropriate U.S. agencies, as noted below.

U.S. Foreign Corrupt Practices Act: In 1977, the United States enacted the Foreign Corrupt Practices Act (FCPA), which makes it unlawful for a U.S. person, and certain foreign issuers of securities, to make a corrupt payment to foreign public officials for the purpose of obtaining or retaining business for or with, or directing business to, any person. The FCPA also applies to foreign firms and persons who take any act in furtherance of such a corrupt payment while in the United States. For more detailed information on the FCPA, see the FCPA Lay-Person's Guide at:
http://www.justice.gov/criminal/fraud/

Other Instruments: It is U.S. Government policy to promote good governance, including host country implementation and enforcement of anti-corruption laws and policies pursuant to their obligations under international agreements. Since enactment of the FCPA, the United States has been instrumental to the expansion of the international framework to fight corruption. Several significant components of this framework are the OECD Convention on Combating Bribery of Foreign Public Officials in International Business Transactions (OECD Antibribery Convention), the United Nations Convention against Corruption (UN Convention), the Inter-American Convention against Corruption (OAS Convention), the Council of Europe Criminal and Civil Law Conventions, and a growing list of U.S. free trade agreements. This country is party to [add instrument to which this country is party], but generally all countries prohibit the bribery and solicitation of their public officials.

OECD Antibribery Convention: The OECD Antibribery Convention entered into force in February 1999. As of December 2009, there are 38 parties to the Convention including the United States (see http://www.oecd.org/dataoecd/59/13/40272933.pdf). Major exporters China, India, and Russia are not parties, although the U.S. Government strongly endorses their eventual accession to the Convention. The Convention obligates the Parties to criminalize bribery of foreign public officials in the conduct of international business. The United States meets its international obligations under the OECD

Antibribery Convention through the U.S. FCPA. Morocco is not a party to the OECD Convention.

UN Convention: The UN Anticorruption Convention entered into force on December 14, 2005, and there are 143 parties to it as of December 2009 (see http://www.unodc.org/unodc/en/treaties/CAC/signatories.html). The UN Convention is the first global comprehensive international anticorruption agreement. The UN Convention requires countries to establish criminal and other offences to cover a wide range of acts of corruption. The UN Convention goes beyond previous anticorruption instruments, covering a broad range of issues ranging from basic forms of corruption such as bribery and solicitation, embezzlement, trading in influence to the concealment and laundering of the proceeds of corruption. The Convention contains transnational business bribery provisions that are functionally similar to those in the OECD Antibribery Convention and contains provisions on private sector auditing and books and records requirements. Other provisions address matters such as prevention, international cooperation, and asset recovery. Morocco is a party to the UN Convention.

 OAS Convention: In 1996, the Member States of the Organization of American States (OAS) adopted the first international anticorruption legal instrument, the Inter-American Convention against Corruption (OAS Convention), which entered into force in March 1997. The OAS Convention, among other things, establishes a set of preventive measures against corruption, provides for the criminalization of certain acts of corruption, including transnational bribery and illicit enrichment, and contains a series of provisions to strengthen the cooperation between its States Parties in areas such as mutual legal assistance and technical cooperation. As of December 2009, the OAS Convention has 33 parties (see http://www.oas.org/juridico/english/Sigs/b-58.html) Morocco is not a party to the OAS Convention.

Council of Europe Criminal Law and Civil Law Conventions: Many European countries are parties to either the Council of Europe (CoE) Criminal Law Convention on Corruption, the Civil Law Convention, or both. The Criminal Law Convention requires criminalization of a wide range of national and transnational conduct, including bribery, money-laundering, and account offenses. It also incorporates provisions on liability of legal persons and witness protection. The Civil Law Convention includes provisions on compensation for damage relating to corrupt acts, whistleblower protection, and validity of contracts, inter alia. The Group of States against Corruption (GRECO) was established in 1999 by the CoE to monitor compliance with these and related anti-corruption standards. Currently, GRECO comprises 46 member States (45 European countries and the United States). As of December 2009, the Criminal Law Convention has 42 parties and the Civil Law Convention has 34 (see www.coe.int/greco). Morocco is not a party to the Council of Europe Conventions.

Free Trade Agreements: While it is U.S. Government policy to include anticorruption provisions in free trade agreements (FTAs) that it negotiates with its trading partners, the anticorruption provisions have evolved over time. The most recent FTAs negotiated now require trading partners to criminalize "active bribery" of public officials (offering bribes to any public official must be made a criminal offense, both domestically and trans-nationally) as well as domestic "passive bribery" (solicitation of a bribe by a domestic official). All U.S. FTAs may be found at the U.S. Trade Representative Website: http://www.ustr.gov/trade-agreements/free-trade-agreements. Morocco has an FTA with the United States: Morocco has a free trade agreement (FTA) in place with the United States, the United States-Morocco FTA which came into force in January 2006.

Local Laws: U.S. firms should familiarize themselves with local anticorruption laws, and, where appropriate, seek legal counsel. While the U.S. Department of Commerce cannot provide legal advice on local laws, the Department's U.S. and Foreign Commercial Service can provide assistance with navigating the host country's legal system and obtaining a list of local legal counsel.

Assistance for U.S. Businesses: The U.S. Department of Commerce offers several services to aid U.S. businesses seeking to address business-related corruption issues. For example, the U.S. and Foreign Commercial Service can provide services that may assist U.S. companies in conducting their due diligence as part of the company's overarching compliance program when choosing business partners or agents overseas. The U.S. Foreign and Commercial Service can be reached directly through its offices in every major U.S. and foreign city, or through its Website at www.trade.gov/cs.

The Departments of Commerce and State provide worldwide support for qualified U.S. companies bidding on foreign government contracts through the Commerce Department's Advocacy Center and State's Office of Commercial and Business Affairs. Problems, including alleged corruption by foreign governments or competitors, encountered by U.S. companies in seeking such foreign business opportunities can be brought to the attention of appropriate U.S. government officials, including local embassy personnel and through the Department of Commerce Trade Compliance Center "Report A Trade Barrier" Website at tcc.export.gov/Report_a_Barrier/index.asp.

Guidance on the U.S. FCPA: The Department of Justice's (DOJ) FCPA Opinion Procedure enables U.S. firms and individuals to request a statement of the Justice Department's present enforcement intentions under the anti-bribery provisions of the FCPA regarding any proposed business conduct. The details of the opinion procedure are available on DOJ's Fraud Section Website at www.justice.gov/criminal/fraud/fcpa. Although the Department of Commerce has no enforcement role with respect to the FCPA, it supplies general guidance to U.S. exporters who have questions about the FCPA and about international developments concerning the FCPA. For further information, see the Office of the Chief Counsel for International Counsel, U.S. Department of Commerce, Website, at http://www.ogc.doc.gov/trans_anti_bribery.html. More general information on the FCPA is available at the Websites listed below.

Exporters and investors should be aware that generally all countries prohibit the bribery of their public officials, and prohibit their officials from soliciting bribes under domestic laws.   Most countries are required to criminalize such bribery and other acts of corruption by virtue of being parties to various international conventions discussed above.

Public sector corruption, including bribery of public officials, remains a major challenge for U.S. firms operating in Morocco. Morocco has a wide body of laws and regulations to combat corruption, but it remains a problem, in part due to the low salaries in the public sector. Prime Minister Abbas El Fassi has made the fight against corruption one of his key priorities. A new anti-corruption agency was set up in 2007 but only became operational in January 2009. Headed by a respected senior Moroccan official who has been active in anti-corruption efforts since the founding of "Transparency Maroc," the agency was created to "moralize" Moroccan public life and to propose specific steps the government can take to address the issue. In 2010, an anti-corruption hotline was introduced under the auspices of the Moroccan employers' federation, CGEM.

In spite of legislative improvements and a slight rebound over last year's 89th place ranking, Morocco's 85th place in Transparency International's 2010 corruption index is still well below its 2002 level, when it was 52nd. Government officials have criticized the Index, which reflects public perceptions concerning corruption, for not emphasizing recent anti-corruption efforts. These include enhancing the transparency of public tenders and implementation of a requirement that senior government officials declare their assets at the start and end of their government service.

Since 2003 Morocco has taken a series of steps to counter terrorist finance, strengthen controls against money laundering, and conform to international accounting and banking standards. Comprehensive anti-money laundering legislation was passed in 2007, and an independent Financial Intelligence Unit became operational in 2009. The legislation draws largely from recommendations made by the Organization for Economic Cooperation and Development's (OECD's) Financial Action Task Force (FATF).

Anti-Corruption Resources

Some useful resources for individuals and companies regarding combating corruption in global markets include the following:

- Information about the U.S. Foreign Corrupt Practices Act (FCPA), including a "Lay-Person's Guide to the FCPA" is available at the U.S. Department of Justice's Website at: http://www.justice.gov/criminal/fraud/fcpa.

- Information about the OECD Antibribery Convention including links to national implementing legislation and country monitoring reports is available at: http://www.oecd.org/department/0,3355,en_2649_34859_1_1_1_1_1,00.html. See also new Antibribery Recommendation and Good Practice Guidance Annex for companies: http://www.oecd.org/dataoecd/11/40/44176910.pdf

- General information about anticorruption initiatives, such as the OECD Convention and the FCPA, including translations of the statute into several languages, is available at the Department of Commerce Office of the Chief Counsel for International Commerce Website: http://www.ogc.doc.gov/trans_anti_bribery.html.

- Transparency International (TI) publishes an annual Corruption Perceptions Index (CPI).   The CPI measures the perceived level of public-sector corruption in 180 countries and territories around the world. The CPI is available at: http://www.transparency.org/policy_research/surveys_indices/cpi/2009.   TI also publishes an annual *Global Corruption Report* which provides a systematic evaluation of the state of corruption around the world. It includes an in-depth analysis of a focal theme, a series of country reports that document major corruption related events and developments from all continents and an overview of the latest research findings on anti-corruption diagnostics and tools. See http://www.transparency.org/publications/gcr.

- The World Bank Institute publishes Worldwide Governance Indicators (WGI). These indicators assess six dimensions of governance in 212 countries, including Voice and Accountability, Political Stability and Absence of Violence, Government Effectiveness, Regulatory Quality, Rule of Law and Control of Corruption. See http://info.worldbank.org/governance/wgi/sc_country.asp. The World Bank Business Environment and Enterprise Performance Surveys may also be of interest and are available at: http://go.worldbank.org/RQQXYJ6210.

- The World Economic Forum publishes the *Global Enabling Trade Report*, which presents the rankings of the Enabling Trade Index, and includes an assessment of the transparency of border administration (focused on bribe payments and corruption) and a separate segment on corruption and the regulatory environment. See http://www.weforum.org/en/initiatives/gcp/GlobalEnablingTradeReport/index.htm.

- Additional country information related to corruption can be found in the U.S. State Department's annual *Human Rights Report* available at http://www.state.gov/g/drl/rls/hrrpt/.

- Global Integrity, a nonprofit organization, publishes its annual *Global Integrity Report*, which provides indicators for 92 countries with respect to governance and anti-corruption. The report highlights the strengths and weaknesses of national level anti-corruption systems. The report is available at: http://report.globalintegrity.org/.

Bilateral Investment Agreements   Return to top

The U.S.-Morocco FTA was signed in June 2004 and came into effect in January 2006, ending tariffs on over 98% of the bilateral trade in consumer and industrial goods and subsuming previous bilateral investment agreements. For more details on the U.S.-Morocco FTA please visit www.moroccousafta.com

OPIC and Other Investment Insurance Programs   Return to top

Morocco's agreement with the Overseas Private Investment Corporation was most recently updated in March 1995. Morocco is also a member of the Kuwait-based Arab Investment Guarantee Organization (OAGI) and the Multilateral Investment Guarantee Agency (MIGA). For more details please see www.opic.gov

Labor   Return to top

Once strong and politically influential, the Moroccan trade union movement is now fragmented and no longer possesses the political clout it carried 50 years ago when it helped lead the country to independence. Nevertheless, 5 of the 24 trade union federations retain the potential to influence political life. Although unions claim high membership rates, Morocco has about 600,000 unionized workers, less than 6% of the 11.26 million workforce.

Moroccan labor law and practice draw from French models. The labor code was reformed in 2004, reducing the maximum workweek from 48 to 44 hours. Labor codes concerning unions and the right to strike do not cover domestic workers. Investors continue to view labor regulations as a significant constraint. They complain that procedures regarding lay-offs remain complicated and onerous, and they impose a significant financial burden on companies. Rules regarding foreign personnel are also vague and can lead to conflicting interpretations and arbitrary decisions.

Morocco has ratified the International Labor Organization (ILO) convention covering the right to organize and bargain collectively, and any group of eight workers can organize. Article 14 of the Constitution gives workers the right to strike, but no detailed law defines it. For a union to engage in collective bargaining it must have at least 35% of the enterprise's workforce as registered members. The Ministry of Interior occasionally intervenes, especially if the Government believes strategic interests are threatened. There are mandatory procedures governing the settlement of disputes, though the Government settles them on a case-by-case basis.

The official national unemployment figure at the end of the third quarter 2010 fell to 9% compared to 9.8% a year earlier. The more meaningful urban unemployment figure improved from 14.8% in 2009 to 13.8% in 2010. The Moroccan High Planning Commission (HCP) claimed that most of these employment gains occurred among urban 15 to 24 year-olds. The minimum wage stands at 10.64 MAD per hour, approximately $1.28 per hour.

Foreign-Trade Zones/Free Ports   Return to top

The industrial free trade zones (FTZs) and Logistic Zones in Tangier have brought foreign investment and employment to the northern region of Morocco. The companies located in the FTZs may import goods duty free and are exempt from other taxes. Moroccan labor laws still apply, but few, if any, firms are unionized. There is also an offshore banking law covering Tangier.

Foreign Direct Investment Statistics   Return to top

The Moroccan foreign exchange office maintains balance of payments statistics that include annual foreign exchange inflows for private foreign investment. These statistics differentiate between foreign direct investment (purchases of companies or increases in capital), portfolio investment, and short-term financing for current account expenditures, e.g. lending to a subsidiary for purchases of equipment. There are no official statistics on the stock of foreign investment in Morocco, but new foreign investment peaked at about $4.6 billion in 2007, before declining to around $3.6 billion in 2008 and $2.5 billion in 2009. The following tables are based on balance of payments statistics.

Foreign Direct Investment in Morocco
(USD Millions)

Year	Total FDI	Percent of GDP
1998	384.6	1.1
1999	945.6	2.7
2000	245.8	0.8
2001	2,732.2	8.0
2002	534.2	1.3
2003	2,430.2	4.9
2004	1,070.5	1.9
2005	3,007.6	5.1
2006	2,962.5	4.5
2007	4,629.2	6.2
2008	3,608.1	4.1
2009	2,510.7	2.75

Foreign Direct Investment Inflows by Country of Origin
(USD Millions)

Country	2005	2006	2007	2008	2009
United States	25.5	98.1	188.2	108.1	79.06
France	2234.6	982.5	1740.7	1360.7	928.2
Spain	162.4	817.2	744.9	337.6	208.12
Germany	96.3	106.8	200.8	169.3	98.05
UK	50.9	105.8	314.2	156.7	128.28
Netherlands	29.3	25.8	61.5	24.3	31.29
Benelux	48.0	296.0	160.7	133.9	*122.93
Saudi Arabia	40.8	37.5	77.6	65.9	32.95
Switzerland	85.4	102.9	161.6	214.3	145.46
UAE	81.9	87.9	464.6	608.5	149.22

Kuwait	25.1	115.0	192.1	14.9	373.98
Italy	23.6	38.0	105.4	99.0	73.83
Portugal	6.8	5.7	6.8	5.8	6.58
Others	97.0	143.0	210.0	309.1	281.97
Total	2962.5	4629.1	3608.1	3007.6	2510.7

N.B	2005	2006	2007	2008	2009
Exchange Rate (MAD/USD)	8.88	8.80	8.20	7.75	8.0846
GDP(Billions of USD)	58.90	65.40	75.10	88.88	91.06

*In 2009, Office des Changes began reporting separately on Belgium and Luxembourg.

Foreign Direct Investment Inflows by Sector
(USD Millions)

Sector	2005	2006	2007	2008	2009
Industry	308.0	1019.6	404.2	230.2	294.5
Tourism	346.9	889.6	1515.0	732.2	380.86
Real Estate	272.8	467.8	925.7	1180.9	725.1
Banking	5.0	166.3	222.4	639.9	489.86
Insurance	128.9	166.2	2.6	25.9	33.82
Commerce	49.7	118.9	41.9	23.2	19.15
Holding	23.6	16.8	103.4	285.1	24.14
Energy and Mining	42.5	11.4	343.7	202.4	10.48
Transport	36.2	6.4	333.8	22.7	51.39
Public Works	18.0	3.9	64.9	32.6	14.46
Telecommunications	1,725.2	3.1	376.5	29.7	369.83
Agriculture	0.1	2.8	4.0	3.5	1.98
Fishing	0.1	0.0	0.5	2.8	0.1

Studies	0.1	0.0	0.0	0.0	0.0
Other Services	46.9	76.8	275.1	192.7	88.27
Other	3.5	12.8	15.6	4.4	6.79
Total	3007.6	2962.5	4629.1	3608.2	2510.7

Major Foreign Investors

U.S.

Industries Marocaines Modernes
Parent company: Procter and Gamble
Sector: Soaps and toiletries
Number of employees: 600

Coca-Cola Export Corporation
Parent company: The Coca-Cola Export Corp.
Number of employees: 5,000

FRI—McDonald's Morocco
Parent company: McDonald's Corporation
Number of employees: 2,000
-Plan to invest nearly $60 million over three years beginning in 2011

MATIS Aerospace
Parent company: Boeing/Royal Air Maroc/Labinal (Joint venture)
Sector: Aerospace production
Number of employees: 580

Delphi Automotive (former division of GM)
Sector: Auto part manufacturer
Number of employees: 4,890
-Present in Tanger-Med Free Trade Auto Zone, produces for export only

Kraft Foods
Sector: Food Products
Number of employees: 200

Cargill
Sector: Food production and distribution
Number of employees: 85
-Recently invested $17 million in a storage facility at the Casablanca port (Silos du Maroc) in partnership with the local railway company

Minco Aviation Electronics
Sector: Aviation/Hi Tech
Number of employees: 66
-Produces for export only

Kerzner International
Parent company: Colony Capital
Sector: Tourism - Mazagan Beach Resort
Number of employees: 1,300

Colgate Palmolive Maroc
Sector: Pharmaceutical and cosmetic
Number of employees: 122

Ecomed
Parent company: The Consortium Global Environmental Sustainability, Inc. (GESI) and
Edgeboro International Inc.
Sector: Waste Management
Number of employees: 70
- Investing about $7.5 million over 10 years in Fes project and about $100 million over
18 years in Casablanca project

CMCP
Parent company: International Paper
Sector: Packing
Number of employees: 1,500

Fruit of the Loom
Sector: Textile
Number of employees: 2,300
-Production of high quality t-shirts for export to European market only

Dell Computers
Sector: Computers/Hi Tech
Number of employees: 1,700

Pfizer
Sector: Pharmaceutical
Number of employees: 151

Brinks
Sector: Security
Number of employees: 1500

Other

DHL (German)
Sector: Packing/Transportation
Number of employees: 300

Jorf Lasfar Energy Company
Parent company: TACA Energy (operated by CMS Energy)
Sector: Independent power project
Number of employees: 317

Lafarge Betons
Parent company: Lafarge (France)
Sector: Concrete
Number of employees: 160

Holcim (Maroc)
Parent company: Holcim (Switzerland)
Sector: Concrete
Number of employees: 501-1,000

Tecmed Maroc
Parent company: Grupo ACS (Spain)
Sector: Waste collection
Number of employees: N/A

Bymaro S.A.
Parent company: Bouygues S.A. (France)
Sector: Construction and civil engineering
Number of employees: 1,500

Renault Maroc
Parent company: Renault S.A. (France)
Sector: Motor vehicle assembly
Number of employees: 285

Alstom Maroc
Parent company: Alstom (France)
Sector: Power generation and transport
Number of employees: N/A

EADS Maroc Aviation
Parent company: European Aeronautic Defense and Space Company (Europe)
Sector: Aeronautics and defense
Number of employees: 251-500

Sanofi-Aventis Maroc
Parent company: Sanofi-Aventis SA (France)
Sector: Pharmaceutical manufacturing
Number of employees: 185

Novartis Pharma Maroc
Parent company: Novartis International AG (Switzerland)
Sector: Pharmaceutical
Number of employees: 180

Nestlé Maroc
Parent company: Nestlé SA (Switzerland)
Sector: Consumer packaged goods
Number of employees: 590

Altadis Maroc
Parent company: Altadis (Spanish)
Sector: Tobacco
Number of employees: 1,000+

Web Resources Return to top

Agence Marocaine de Développement des Investissements:
www.invest.gov.ma

AmCham Morocco Trade & Investment Guide:
http://www.moroccousafta.com/index_ang.htm

Return to table of contents

Chapter 7: Trade and Project Financing

- How Do I Get Paid (Methods of Payment)
- How Does the Banking System Operate
- Foreign-Exchange Controls
- U.S. Banks and Local Correspondent Banks
- Project Financing
- Web Resources

How Do I Get Paid (Methods of Payment)   Return to top

To pay for imports of goods and services into Morocco, local importers do not need an authorization from the Foreign Exchange Office. In accordance with Article VIII of the International Monetary Fund statute dealing with convertibility for the current transactions, and in line with the Moroccan liberalization measures initiated in 1993, the Foreign Exchange Office delegated to Moroccan-authorized banks to "freely carry out settlements relating to imports, exports, international transport, insurance and reinsurance, foreign technical assistance, travel, schooling, medical care, savings on income, as well as all the other operations considered as current."

According to regulations governing foreign exchange, payment of goods imported into Morocco is processed only after the actual entrance of the goods into Morocco. Buyers are allowed to prepay up to 40% of the invoice amount. Banks are authorized to open letters of credit and/or to accept bills of exchange. The letters of credit must include a special clause that stipulates that the "payment is subject to justification of direct and exclusive shipment of goods to Morocco." The transport documents justifying the shipment are: the freight bill, airway bill, bill of lading, document of combined means of transportation, or receipt from Post office for mail parcels.

In 2007, the Foreign Exchange Office initiated a liberalization program concerning foreign exchange operations related to different sectors including international trade. Complete prepayment is now allowed for import of goods with a FOB value under 200,000 dirhams ($24,351 in February 2011). The Foreign Exchange Office regulations also allow for advance payments not exceeding 40% of the FOB value of imports of capital equipment.

Banks are authorized to issue bank guarantees to secure payments to foreign suppliers. Importers normally give local buyers up to 90-days' credit.

http://www.oc.gov.ma/Circulaires/Import/1718.asp

How Does the Banking System Operate
Return to top

In comparison to the rest of the Arab world and Africa, Morocco continues to modernize its relatively comprehensive banking system, originally modeled after the French system. There are 16 banks in the country plus five government-owned specialized financial institutions, about 30 credit agencies and about 12 leasing companies. The bank reform law of 1993 laid out parameters for banking activities, clarified oversight and control responsibilities, specified legal penalties for violations of banking regulations and established a deposit guarantee fund. Pending banking reform legislation will further liberalize the sector and improve oversight coordination and lines of authority.

Since financial liberalization, credit is allocated freely, and the central bank has used indirect methods to control the interest rate and volume of credit. The banking system is still used by the government to channel domestic savings to finance government debt, and banks are required to hold part of their assets in bonds paying below market interest rates.

Morocco's banking sector is stronger, and the private sector's role is more active, than in many other African countries. The potential in this sector is great, as it is estimated that only 47% of the population use banks.

The Casablanca Stock Exchange is one of the largest and most important in Africa. Privatized in 1996, the CSE is managed by 13 brokerage companies and regulated by an independent oversight commission similar to the SEC.

For more information on foreign exchange, please see below and check "Efficient Capital Markets" under Chapter 6.

Foreign-Exchange Controls
Return to top

Morocco maintains a system of foreign exchange controls managed by the Foreign Exchange Office (Office des Changes), but the rules on transfers have been progressively liberalized to the point where the dirham is freely convertible according to the IMF definition for current account transactions. The value of the dirham is tied to a basket of hard currencies weighted according to Morocco's foreign trade. Because this basket is dominated by the Euro, variations in the dollar/euro rates are generally reflected in the dirham's dollar value.

Authority to buy and sell foreign exchange has been delegated to the banking system, which will carry out transactions on presentation of appropriate documentation justifying the transaction such as an invoice to pay for imports. Capital transactions require authorization from the Foreign Exchange Office and are routinely granted for business-related transactions. Under the Moroccan investment code, the government guarantees repatriation of both invested capital and profits, provided that the initial capital investment was filed and registered.

Local Correspondent Banks:
Banque Marocaine du Commerce Exterieur (BMCE)
Banque Centrale Populaire (BCP)
Attijariwafa Bank
Banque Marocaine du Commerce et de l'Industrie (BMCI)
Crédit du Maroc (CDM)
Société Générale Marocaine de Banques (SGMB)

U.S. Banks with Moroccan Branches:
Citibank Maghreb (Citi-Group)

The principal multilateral financial institutions such as the World Bank, the IFC, the African Development Bank, and the European Investment Bank all lend to Morocco for infrastructure development.

The Commerce Department's Office of Multilateral Development Bank Operations (MDBO) provides one-stop shopping services to U.S. firms interested in doing business with the MDBs. Its staff can help U.S. companies learn about opportunities and projects financed by the multilateral development banks. For more information on any of these services in the U.S., contact MDBO at (202) 482-3399 or fax (202) 273-0927 or the Commercial Service Liaison Staff, Office of the U.S. Executive Director, the World Bank, 1818 H Street NW, Washington DC 20433, USA. Tel: (202) 458-0118/0120, Fax: (202) 477-2967.

The International Finance Corporation (IFC), a private-sector lending arm of the World Bank, has cooperative agreements with Moroccan institutions and can provide services including financing from commercial banks, export credit agencies and other institutions. Contact in Morocco: Joumana Cobein Country Manager, IFC, 7 rue Larbi Ben Abdellah, Rabat. Tel: (212) 537 63 24 79; Fax: (212) 537 63 60 50. For more information on opportunities for U.S. firms, click http://www.ifc.org

The Multilateral Investment Guarantee Agency (MIGA) is part of the World Bank group. Its purpose is to encourage foreign direct investment in developing countries by providing investors with political risk insurance. Like its counterpart OPIC, MIGA provides insurance to cover the risk of currency transfer, expropriation, war and civil disturbance, and breach of contract by the host government. Morocco is a member of MIGA. Contact: Multilateral Investment Guarantee Agency, 1818 H Street, NW, Washington, DC 20433, and Guarantees Dept. Tel: (202) 473-6168. For more information on opportunities for U.S. firms, click http://www.miga.org

Types of Available Export Financing and Insurance:

(1) The U.S. Small Business Administration (SBA) has a number of programs targeted toward helping small and medium-sized companies to develop export markets. In particular, the SBA offers an export working capital guarantee program whereby the SBA

will guarantee up to 75% of a bank loan to provide working capital or a line of credit to exporters. This enables exporters to offer more favorable payment terms to their Moroccan buyers or provide working capital while export orders are being manufactured. Contact: U.S. Small Business Administration, Office of International Trade, 409 Third Street, SW, Washington, DC 20416, Tel. (202) 205-6720, Fax (202) 205-7272, or call 1-800-USA-TRADE for the location of the nearest U.S. Export Assistance Center.

(2) The U.S. Export-Import Bank promotes the exports through loans, guarantees, and insurance programs, all of which are available in Morocco. Ex-Im Bank can guarantee U.S. commercial bank financing for U.S. exporters. Its export insurance programs provide insurance coverage against the risk of default on foreign receivables. However, a Moroccan guarantee, either from the government or private bank, may also be required. Ex-Im Bank has a small bundling facility (guaranteed credits of $10 million) with Credit du Maroc, the Moroccan subsidiary of Credit Lyonnais France. In 2006, Ex-Im Bank signed an MOU with Attijariwafa Bank to support increased U.S. exports to Morocco. Contact: Export-Import Bank, 811 Vermont Ave., NW, Washington, DC 20871; 1-800-565-3946; Regional Manager for North Africa and the Middle East, Tel: (202) 565-3716; Fax: (202) 565-3931; International Lending Fax: (202) 565-3816.

(3) The U.S. Trade and Development Agency (USTDA) is an independent U.S. government agency that promotes U.S. exports for major development projects in middle-income and developing countries. USTDA funds feasibility studies, technical assistance, orientation visits and other project planning services related to major projects. Consulting contracts must be awarded to U.S. companies. U.S. involvement in project planning helps position U.S. suppliers for follow-on contracts when projects are implemented. USTDA is active in Morocco in energy, telecommunications, tourism, chemicals, water, environmental, railway, port and airport sectors. Contact: U.S. Trade and Development Agency, Heather Lanigan, Country Manager, Room 309 SA-16, Washington, D.C. 20523-1602; Tel: (703) 875-4357; Fax: (703) 875-4009.

Web Resources   Return to top

Export-Import Bank of the United States: http://www.exim.gov

Country Limitation Schedule: http://www.exim.gov/tools/country/country_limits.html

OPIC: http://www.opic.gov

Trade and Development Agency: http://www.tda.gov/

SBA's Office of International Trade: http://www.sba.gov/oit/

USDA Commodity Credit Corporation: http://www.fsa.usda.gov/ccc/default.htm

U.S. Agency for International Development: http://www.usaid.gov

African Development Bank: http://www.afdb.org/en/countries/north-africa/morocco/

Return to table of contents

Return to table of contents

Chapter 8: Business Travel

- Business Customs
- Travel Advisory
- Visa Requirements
- Telecommunications
- Transportation
- Language
- Health
- Local Time, Business Hours and Holidays
- Temporary Entry of Materials and Personal Belongings
- Web Resources

Business Customs Return to top

Moroccan business representatives are increasingly interested in exploring business ventures with U.S. companies. Implementation of the FTA has opened new sectors and attracted a large number of U.S. firms to explore the local market. Nevertheless, there are still many subtle cultural differences that must be overcome to succeed in this market.

A primary difference is the business culture. Many of Morocco's leading industrialists and businesspersons were educated in Europe. Morocco is a former French protectorate and many of its business practices are based on the French system. The main language used in business discussions is French. Both public and private procurements are predominantly in French with some exceptions.

Moroccans are increasingly interested in doing business with U.S. firms in part because it makes good business sense to diversify. The value of the Euro compared with the U.S. dollar creates opportunities for U.S. firms to engage in new business dialogue. A growing number of young, talented U.S.-educated entrepreneurs returning to Morocco are contributing to an improved receptivity for U.S. firms and U.S. business culture.

Many aspects of Morocco's rich culture and heritage are absorbed in its business etiquette, and U.S. business representatives should make every effort to understand the subtleties of this important aspect of doing business in Morocco. For example it is always polite to accept an invitation to drink tea or coffee. It is wise to build trust and friendship in order to build the business. That said, businesses should be wary of agreeing or entering into any "informal" business ventures and vet all proposals and document all commitments. Verbal agreements, which are common in Morocco, will not hold up in court.

When planning a business trip to Morocco, consult with a U.S. Commercial Service Trade Specialist and the Commercial Section at the U.S. Consulate General in

Casablanca, Morocco to receive value-added advice, trade leads, contacts, or matchmaking services: http://www.buyusa.gov/morocco/en/

Businesses are open Monday through Friday and sometimes Saturday morning. Most businesses close for lunch from noon to 2:00 p.m., except during the month of Ramadan, when they remain open at mid-day but close earlier in the afternoon. Morocco is a predominantly Muslim country. Thus many local establishments refrain from serving any alcoholic beverages during the holy month of Ramadan. Please check other religious holidays listed under the Business Travel section.

Travel Advisory   Return to top

For current travel information, refer to http://morocco.usembassy.gov/ or Country Specific Information for Morocco: http://travel.state.gov/travel/cis_pa_tw/cis/cis_975.html

Current Travel Warnings: http://travel.state.gov/travel/cis_pa_tw/tw/tw_1764.html

U.S. Citizens traveling in Morocco may want to register via this website: https://travelregistration.state.gov/ibrs/ui/

Visa Requirements   Return to top

In general, a tourist visa, which is valid for a period of three months, is the only type of temporary visa issued for Morocco. U.S. citizens and European Union member countries do not need a visa for entry into Morocco. Entry visas are required for foreign nationals from certain countries, including Egypt, Iran, Sudan and Syria. A residence permit is required to stay in Morocco for more than 90 days.

Moroccan representatives of U.S. companies that require travel to the United States should allow sufficient time for visa issuance. U.S. business visa applicants should go to the following link: http://morocco.usembassy.gov/visas/nonimmigrant-visas.html

U.S. Companies that require travel of foreign businesspersons to the United States should be advised that security evaluations are handled via an interagency process. Visa applicants should go to the following links.

State Department Visa Website: http://travel.state.gov/visa/

The Consular Section of the U.S. Embassy: http://morocco.usembassy.gov/

Telecommunications Return to top

The telephone system has greatly improved in recent years. The national telecommunications network offers a range of services including cellular, paging, video conferencing, voice mail and Internet. Most U.S. phones will be able to roam in Morocco and vice-versa.

Transportation Return to top

Morocco has made the development of its communication and transportation networks a top priority. Morocco's infrastructure for the distribution of goods and services is good and will continue to improve as the government nears completion on several projects. Morocco's road network is among the best in Africa. Most parts of the country are readily accessible by well-surfaced roads. Most agricultural and manufactured goods move by road. Casablanca's Mohammed V Airport is the largest airport in Morocco. It offers 50 flights a day to the United States, Europe, the Middle East and elsewhere in Africa. The railway network handles passenger service and the freight service of phosphates, fertilizers, chemical products and other minerals. The port of Casablanca, the second largest in Africa, handles 40% of all goods imported and/or exported. Morocco's shipping costs are high in comparison to its Mediterranean competitors. There is frequent ferry service to and from Spain, France and Italy for tourists.

Language Return to top

Modern Standard Arabic is the official language, but the local dialect, called Darija, Western Arabic or "arabe dialectal," is the vernacular. It differs substantially from Modern Standard Arabic, both in pronunciation and vocabulary.

French is fairly prevalent, especially among the educated classes and the older generations. In the north of Morocco, Spanish is quite common.

A growing number of young Moroccan entrepreneurs with degrees from U.S. schools conduct business in English; nevertheless, it is always a good idea to determine in advance the language to be used during a meeting should it be necessary to hire an interpreter. Generally, business meetings are conducted in French.

Health Return to top

MEDICAL FACILITIES: Adequate medical care is available in Morocco's largest cities, particularly in Rabat and Casablanca, although not all facilities meet Western standards. Specialized care or treatment may not be available. Medical facilities are adequate for non-emergency matters, particularly in the urban areas, but most medical staff will have limited or no English skills. Emergency and specialized care outside the major cities is far below U.S. standards, and in many instances may not be available at all. Travelers planning to drive in the mountains and other remote areas may wish to carry a medical kit for emergencies. In the event of car accidents involving injuries, immediate ambulance service usually is not available.

Persons taking medication are advised to bring enough to last during their stay in Morocco. Moroccan customs and health authorities will not release medication sent through the mail.

Useful information is available in the U.S. Embassy Morocco website. http://morocco.usembassy.gov/service/professional-services/medical-information.html

Local Time, Business Hours, and Holidays   Return to top

Morocco is on Greenwich Mean Time (GMT). The time difference between Morocco and the East Coast is 5 hours and West Coast 8 hours during Standard Time months.

Holidays in 2011:

December 31	New Year 2011
January 11	Presentation of Moroccan Independence Proclamation
January 17	Martin Luther King Day
February 16/17	Prophet's Birthday (*)
February 21	President's Day
May 1	Moroccan Labor Day
May 30	Memorial Day
July 4	U.S. Independence Day
July 30	Feast of the Throne
August 20	Revolution of the King and the People
August 21	King's Birthday
Aug 31 & September 1	Aid Al Fitr (end of Ramadan) (*)
September 5	U.S. Labor Day
October 10	Columbus Day
November 7& 8	Aid Al Adha (*)
November 11	Veteran's Day
November 18	Feast of Independence
November 24	Thanksgiving Day
November 27	First of Moharram - Muslim's New Year (*)
December 26	Christmas Day

Table of holidays observed by U.S. mission in Morocco

Note: Holidays with (*) are based on the lunar calendar and change every year. Dates shown are those projected for the year 2011. As is the case in most Muslim countries, it may be more difficult to make business appointments and contacts in Morocco during the month of Ramadan, which will start this year in early August. It is also important to keep in mind that many local businesses shut down for a lengthy period during the summer holidays, e.g. July-August.

Temporary Entry of Materials and Personal Belongings Return to top

Customs may authorize temporary entry of goods on an individual basis. The limit for temporary entry is six months, renewable for up to two years.

Web Resources Return to top

http://morocco.usembassy.gov/

Return to table of contents

Return to table of contents

Chapter 9: Contacts, Market Research and Trade Events

- Contacts
- Market Research
- Trade Events

Contacts Return to top

U.S. EMBASSY RABAT

Ambassador Samuel L. Kaplan
Address: 2, Avenue Mohamed El Fassi (formerly Ave de Marrakesh)
Rabat, Morocco
Tel: (212) (0) 537-76-22-65
http://morocco.usembassy.gov/

Judith A. Chammas, Deputy Chief of Mission
Address: 2, Avenue Mohamed El Fassi (formerly Ave de Marrakesh)
Rabat, Morocco
Tel: (212) (0) 537-76-22-65
Fax: (212) (0) 537-76-56-61
http://morocco.usembassy.gov/

U.S. CONSULATE GENERAL CASABLANCA

Elisabeth Millard, Consul General
8, Bd. Moulay Youssef
Casablanca, Morocco
Tel: (212) (0) 522-26-45-50
http://morocco.usembassy.gov/

Jane Kitson, Senior Commercial Officer (Morocco and Tunisia)
U.S. Commercial Service
8, Bd. Moulay Youssef
Casablanca, Morocco
Tel: (212) (0) 522-26-45-50
http://www.buyusa.gov/morocco/en/

AMERICAN CHAMBER OF COMMERCE (AmCham)

Contact: Pascal Houdayer, President
Rabia El-Alama, Program Director
67, Boulevard Massira Al Khadra
Third Floor, Apt. 6
Casablanca, Morocco
Tel: (212) (0) 522-25-07-36
Fax: (212) (0) 522-25-07-30
Email: amcham@amcham-morocco.com

FINANCIAL SERVICES VOLUNTEER CORPS

William C. Fellows, Regional Director
26 Bl Al Massira El Khadra 3e Etage
Maarif
20100 Casablanca, Morocco
Tel: +212 (0) 522-95-31-20
Fax: +212 (0) 522-39-38-40
Email: wfellows@fsvc.org

MOROCCAN GOVERNMENT AGENCIES

Ministry of Economic and General Affairs
(Ministère des Affaires Economiques et Générales)
Contact: Monkid Mestassi, Deputy Minister
Rabat, Morocco
Tel: 212 (0) 537-77-17-16
Fax: 212 (0) 537-77-47-76
http://www.finances.gov.ma

Ministry of Tourism
(Ministère du Tourisme)
Contact: Yassir Zenagui, Minister
Quartier Administratif
Rabat, Morocco
Tel: (212) (0) 537-56-37-25
Fax: (212) (0) 537-71-70-28
http://www.tourisme-marocain.com

Customs Office
(Direction Des Douanes et Impôts Indirects)
Contact: Zouheir Chorfi, Director
Avenue Annakhil, Centre des Affaires, Hay Riad
Rabat, Morocco
Tel: (212) (0) 537-57-90-11
Fax: (212) (0) 537-71-78-14
E-mail: adii@douane.msie.gov.ma
http://www.douane.gov.ma

Government Agency in charge of the Northern Region
(Agence du Nord)
Contact: Fouad Brini, Managing Director
22, Av. Omar Ibn El Khattab Agdal
Rabat, Morocco
Tel: (212) (0) 537-77-60-13
Fax: (212) (0) 537-77-60-46

Department of Statistics
(Direction des Statistiques)
Contact: Mr. Toufiq Cherkaoui
Rue Mohamed Bel Hassan El Ouazzani
Haut Agdal
Rabat, Morocco
Tel: (212) (0) 661-28-46-92
Fax: (212) (0) 537-77-32-17

Ministry of Industry, Commerce and New Technologies
(Ministère de l'Industrie, du Commerce, et de la Mise à Niveau de l'Economie)
Contact: Ahmed Reda Chami, Minister
Quartier Administratif - Chellah
Rabat, Morocco
Tel: (212) (0) 537-76-45-18
Fax: (212) (0) 537-76-35-37
http://www.mcinet.gov.ma

Ministry of Economy and Finance
(Ministère de L'Economie et des Finances)
Contact: Salaheddine Mezouar, Minister
Contact: Mohamed Chafiki, Chef de Cabinet
Ancien Quartier Administratif
Rabat, Morocco
Tel: (212) (0) 537-76-11-13
Fax: (212) (0) 537-76-50-68

Investment Office
(Direction des Investissements)
Contact: Hassan Bernoussi, Director
32 Rue Honain, Angle rue Michlifen
Agdal
Rabat, Morocco
Tel: (212) (0) 537-67-33-75
Fax: (212) (0) 537-67-34-19
http://www.invest-in-morocco.gov.ma/

Ministry of Agriculture and Fisheries
(Ministère de l'Agriculture, et de la Pêche Maritime)
Contact: M. Aziz Akhannouch, Minister
Quartier Administratif, Chellah
Rabat, Morocco

Tel: (212) (0) 537-76-07-07/537-76-26-36
Fax: (212) (0) 537-76-33-78
http://www.marocagriculture.com/ministere-de-lagriculture-et-de-la-peche-maritime.html

Ministry of Foreign Trade
(Ministère du Commerce Extérieur)
Contact: M. Abdellatif Mazouz, Minister
63 Avenue Moulay Youssef
Rabat, Morocco
Tel: (212) (0) 537-73-56-37
Fax: (212) (0) 537-73-51-43

National Office of Electricity
(Office National de l' Electricité or ONE)
Contact: Ali Fassi Fihri, General Manager
65 Rue Othman Ben Affane
Casablanca, Morocco
Tel: (212) (0) 522-66-80-80
Fax: (212) (0) 522-20-56-98
http://www.one.org.ma

National Regulatory Agency for Telecommunications
(Agence Nationale de Réglementation des Télécommunications or ANRT)
Contact: Azdine El Mountassir Billah, General Manager
Centre d'Affaires B.P 2939
Aile Nord
Hay Riad
Rabat, Morocco
Tel: (212) (0) 537-71-84-00/537-71-86-01
Fax: (212) (0) 537- 20 38 62
http://www.anrt.net.ma/

National Telephone Company
(Maroc Telecom, IAM)
Contact: Abdeslam Ahizoune, President
Avenue Annakhil, Hay-Riad
Rabat, Morocco
Tel: (212) (0) 537-71-41-41
Fax: (212) (0) 537-71-66-66
http://www.iam.net.ma/

National Office of Potable Water
(Office National de l'Eau Potable, ONEP)
Contact: Ali Fassi Fihri, General Manager
Station de Traitement Bouregreg
Avenue Akrach
Rabat, Morocco
Tel: (212) (0) 537-65-06-95 or 96
Fax: (212) (0) 537-65-06-40
http://www.onep.ma/

National Office of Phosphates
(Office Cherifien des Phosphates or OCP)
Contact: Mustapha Terrab, General Manager
Bd. de la Grande Ceinture
Route d'El Jadida
Casablanca, Morocco
Tel: (212) (0) 522-22-23-00
Fax: (212) (0) 522-25-09-99
http://www.ocpgroup.ma/

Moroccan Ports Authority
Societe d'Exploitation des Ports (Sodep, also known as Marsa Maroc)
Contact: Mohamed Abdeljalil, General Manager
175 Bd. Mohamed Zerktouni
Casablanca, Morocco
Tel: (212) (0) 522-23-23-24
Fax: (212) (0) 522-25-81-58
http://www.marsamaroc.co.ma

National Airline Company
(Royal Air Maroc or RAM)
Contact: Driss Benhima, President
Aeroport d'Anfa
Casablanca, Morocco
Tel: (212) (0) 522-91-20-21 or 522-91-20-22
Fax: (212) (0) 522-91-20-95
http://www.royalairmaroc.com/

Bureau of Mining and Oil Exploration Research
(Office Nationale des Hydrocarbures et des Mines or ONHYM)
Contact: Amina Benkhadra
34 Avenue Al Fadila
B.P. 8030
Rabat, Morocco
Tel: (212) (0) 537-28-16-16
Fax: (212) (0) 537-28-16-34
http://www.onhym.com

Country Trade Associations

Moroccan Employers Association
(Confederation Générale des Entreprises du Maroc or CGEM)
Contact: Mohamed Horani, President
23, Boulevard Mohamed Abdou
Casablanca, Morocco
Tel: (212) (0) 522- 99-70-00
Fax: (212) (0) 522- 98-39-71

Moroccan Association of Textiles and Apparel Manufacturers
(Association Marocaine des industries de textile or AMITH))
Mr. Mohamed Tazi, Secretary General
92 Boulevard Moulay Rachid, Casablanca
http://www.textile.ma/amith
Tel: (212) (0) 522-94-81-86
Fax: (212) (0) 522-94-05-87
Email: mtazi@amith.org.ma

Feed Millers Association (AFAC)
Ibrahim Assimi, President
123 Bd Imile Zola
Casablanca, Morocco
Tel: (212) (0) 522-31-12-49 or 522-44-22-76
Fax: (212) (0) 522-442-2-76
Email: fisa@iam.net.ma
http://www.fisa.org.ma

Telecommunications and Computers Association (APEBI)
Contact: Abdallah Deguig, President
17, rue Najib Mahfoud, Quartier Gauthier.
Casablanca, Morocco
Tel: (212) (0) 522-27-47-57
Fax: (212) (0) 522-27-47-28
http://www.apebi.org.ma

Mining Industry Association
(Fédération de l'Industrie Minière)
Minister Amina Benkhadra
1 Place de l'Istiqlal
Casablanca, Morocco
Tel: (212) (0) 522-30-68-98
Fax: (212) (0) 522-31-99-96

Association of Moroccan Importers of Agricultural Equipment
(Association des Marchands et Importateurs de Matériel Agricole- AMIMA)
Chakib Ben El Khadir, President
Zone Industrielle Ouled Salah lot 1711, Bouskoura
Casablanca, Morocco
Tel: (212) (0) 522-65-46-00
Fax: (212) (0) 522-33-45-73

Engineering Association
(Association Marocaine du Conseil et de l'Ingenierie)
Benyahia Noureddine, President
5 Rue Idriss Alakbar
Quartier Hassan
Rabat, Morocco
Tel: (212) (0) 537-70-42-24
Fax: (212) (0) 537-20-03-47
E-mail: fmciass@maghrebnet.net.ma

Specialized Agricultural Trade Associations

Poultry Feed, Poultry, and Eggs Federation
(Fédération Interprofessionnelle du Secteur Agricole or FISA)
Contact: Moulay Youssef Alaoui, President
123, Boulevard Emile Zola
Casablanca, Morocco
Tel: (212) (0) 522-31-12-49
Fax: (212) (0) 522-44-22-76
Email: fisa@iam.net.ma

Feed Manufacturers Association
(Association des Fabricants d'Aliments Composes or AFAC)
Dr. Brahim Assimi
123, Boulevard Emile Zola
Casablanca, Morocco
Tel: (212) (0) 522-31-12-49 or 522-44-22-76
Fax: (212) (0) 522-31-12-49 or 522-44-22-76
http://www.fisa.org.ma

Grains and Pulses Importers and Traders Association
(Association des Negociants en Céréales et Legumineuses or ANCL)
M. Bouchaib El Haddaj, CEO
193, Avenue Hassan II
Casablanca, Morocco
Tel: (212) (0) 522-47-64-38 or 522-47-64-68
Fax: (212) (0) 522-47-42-07
Email: fncl@wanadoo.net.ma

Purebred Dairy Cattle Association
(Association Nationale des Eleveurs de Bovins de Races Pures or ANEB)
M. A. Lomri, Directeur
5, Rue Mohamed Triki, Residence Tissir, Im. B. Apt. 2
Agdal
Rabat, Morocco
Tel: (212) (0) 537-23-02-44
Fax: (212) (0) 537-23-02-62
Email: aneb@menara.ma

Wheat Millers Federation
(Fédération Nationale de la Minoterie or FNM)
M. Ahmed Bouaida, President
Angle Ibn Majid Bahar & Brihmi El Idrissi (Ex Girardot/Havre)
Casablanca, Morocco
Tel: (212) (0) 522-30-18-01 or 522-30-11-58 or 522-30-18-01
Fax: (212) (0) 522 30 65 51/522 30 59 13/522 30 65 51
Email: fnm@wanadoo.net.ma

Office of Trade Events of Casablanca
(Office des Foires et des Expositions de Casablanca or OFEC)
Rue Tiznit, Face à la Mosquée Hassan II
Casablanca 20000, Morocco
Tel (212) (0) 522-27-32-82 or 522-27-16-64 or 522-20-06-54
Fax: (212) (0) 522-27-49-73 or 522-26-49-49
Email: foire@ofec.co.ma
http://www.ofec.co.ma/

Multilateral Development Banks and Trade Assistance Offices

International Finance Corporation
Joumana Cobein, Representative in Morocco
7, Rue Larbi Benabdellah
Rabat, Morocco
Tel: (212) (0) 537-63-60-49
Fax: (212) (0) 537-65-24-79
http://www.ifc.org

World Bank Representation in Morocco
Simon Grey, Country Manager
7, Rue Larbi Benabdellah
Rabat, Morocco
Tel: (212) (0) 537-63-60-50
Fax: (212) (0) 537-63-60-51
http://www.worldbank.org.ma

Washington-Based U.S. Government Contacts

U.S. Department Of Commerce
Christian Reed, Regional Director for ANESA
U.S. Commercial Service, Tel: 202-482-4836, Fax: 202-482-5179
Christopher Wilken, Morocco Desk Officer, Market Access and Compliance
Tel: 202-482-2680 / Fax: 202-482-0878

Amy Tabine, International Trade Specialist, Advocacy Center
Tel: 202-482-5578 / Fax: 202-482-3508

Commercial Law Development Program
Office of the General Counsel
Marc Tejtel, Regional Director
Tel: 202-482-2400
Fax: 202-482-0006
Email: mtejtel@doc.gov

Trade Promotion Coordinating Committee (TPCC) Trade Information Center
Will Center, World Bank Liaison Officer
Tel: 1-800-USA-TRADE
Multilateral Development Banks Office
Tel: 202-458-0120
http://www.worldbank.org/

U.S. Department Of State

William Roebuck, Director of Maghreb Affairs
Molly Hayes, Morocco Desk Officer
Tel: 202-647-1724 / Fax: 202-736-4458

J. Frank Mermoud, Special Representative
Office of the Coordinator for Business Affairs
Tel: 202-647-4675 or 202-647-1625
Fax: 202-636-4458

U.S. Department of Agriculture, Foreign Agriculture Service
Kimberly Svec, Area Director for Africa and Middle East
Tel. 202-690-4066

U.S. Export Import Bank (Ex-Im)

John Richter, Middle East & North Africa Regional Director
Tel: 202-565-3911
Fax: 202-565-3931
http://www.exim.gov/

Overseas Private Investment Corporation (OPIC)

Bruce Cameron, North Africa Desk Office
Tel: 202-336-8799
Tel. Facts Line: 202-336-8700
Fax: 202-408-9859
http://www.opic.gov

U.S. Trade Development Agency
Heather Lanigan, Country Manager for Morocco
Tel: 703-875-4357
Fax: 703-875-4009
http://www.ustda.gov/

Moroccan Embassy in Washington

Aziz Mekouar, Ambassador
Adil Embarch, Economic Officer
1821 Jefferson Place, NW,
Washington, D.C. 20036
Tel: 202-462-7722
Fax: 202-452-0106
E-Mail: aembarch@embassyofmorocco.us

Market Research	Return to top

To view market research reports produced by the U.S. Commercial Service please go to the following website: http://www.export.gov/mrktresearch/index.asp and click on Country and Industry Market Reports.

Please note that these reports are only available to U.S. citizens and U.S. companies. Registration to the site is required, and is free.

Trade Events	Return to top

Please click on the link below for information on upcoming trade events.

http://www.export.gov/tradeevents/index.asp

http://www.buyusa.gov/morocco/en/trade_events.html

Return to table of contents

Return to table of contents

Chapter 10: Guide to Our Services

The President's National Export Initiative aims to double exports over five years by marshaling Federal agencies to **prepare U.S. companies to export successfully, connect them with trade opportunities** and **support them once they do have exporting opportunities**.

The U.S. Commercial Service offers customized solutions to help U.S. exporters, particularly small and medium sized businesses, successfully expand exports to new markets. Our global network of trade specialists will work one-on-one with you through every step of the exporting process, helping you to:

- Target the best markets with our world-class research
- Promote your products and services to qualified buyers
- Meet the best distributors and agents for your products and services
- Overcome potential challenges or trade barriers
- Gain access to the full range of U.S. government trade promotion agencies and their services, including export training and potential trade financing sources

To learn more about the Federal Government's trade promotion resources for new and experienced exporters, please click on the following link: www.export.gov

For more information on the services the U.S. Commercial Service offers to U.S. exporters, please click on the following link: (Insert link to Products and Services section of local buyusa.gov website here.)

U.S. exporters seeking general export information/assistance or country-specific commercial information can also contact the **U.S. Department of Commerce's Trade Information Center** at **(800) USA-TRAD(E).**

We value your feedback on the format and contents of this report. Please send your comments and recommendations to: Market_Research_Feedback@trade.gov

Return to table of contents

www.ingramcontent.com/pod-product-compliance
Lightning Source LLC
Chambersburg PA
CBHW081218170526
45165CB00009B/2861